Your World L

Perfect for K–12 world language teachers, this book provides clear, fun and practical guidance on how to help students master language in the classroom using technology tools. Regardless of your level of technological proficiency as a teacher, this book will show you how to provide effective learning to students in in-person, online and hybrid environments and help you become more comfortable at using digital tools. With teacher vignettes sprinkled throughout, chapters are filled with ideas that will help you foster an inclusive, positive and student-centered classroom environment that supports students' communication skills and social and emotional needs. Poth's easy-to-use methods and strategies will help you create authentic, purposeful learning experiences that will prepare students to be risk-takers in a new language in and beyond the classroom.

Rachelle Dené Poth is a Spanish and STEAM teacher in Oakmont, PA. She is also an attorney, consultant and presenter. You can follow her on Twitter and Instagram at @Rdene915.

Other Eye on Education Books Available from Routledge

(www.routledge.com/eyeoneducation)

Enlivening Instruction with Drama and Improv: A Guide for Second Language and World Language Teachers
Melisa Cahnmann-Taylor and Kathleen R. McGovern

Leading Your Language Program: Strategies for Design and Supervision, Even If You Don't Speak the Language
Catherine Ritz

Rigor in the Remote Learning Classroom Instructional Tips and Strategies
Barbara R. Blackburn

Thriving as an Online K-12 Educator Essential Practices from the Field
Jody Peerless Green

10 Perspectives on Learning in Education
Jimmy Casas, Todd Whitaker, and Jeffrey Zoul

The World Language Teacher's Guide to Active Learning: Strategies and Activities for Increasing Student Engagement
Deborah Blaz

The Genius Hour Guidebook: Fostering Passion, Wonder, and Inquiry in the Classroom
Denise Krebs and Gallit Zvi

From Texting to Teaching Grammar Instruction in a Digital Age
Jeremy Hyler and Troy Hicks

Your World Language Classroom

Strategies for In-Person and Digital Instruction

Rachelle Dené Poth

NEW YORK AND LONDON

First published 2022
by Routledge
605 Third Avenue, New York, NY 10158

and by Routledge
2 Park Square, Milton Park, Abingdon, Oxon, OX14 4RN

Routledge is an imprint of the Taylor & Francis Group, an informa business

Library of Congress Cataloging-in-Publication Data
A catalog record for this book has been requested

ISBN: 978-0-367-68467-9 (hbk)
ISBN: 978-0-367-67913-2 (pbk)
ISBN: 978-1-003-13766-5 (ebk)

DOI: 10.4324/9781003137665

Typeset in Palatino
by Apex CoVantage, LLC

Contents

Meet the Author vi

Introduction 1

1 Building Relationships and Future-Ready Skills/Designing Our Classroom Space 7

2 Low Tech, High Tech, No Tech: Learning for All 29

3 Fostering Strong Communication Skills in Our Students 57

4 Breaking Tradition: If You Are Doing This, Then Try This Instead 88

5 Student-Led Classrooms: Stepping Aside and Letting Students Learn and Lead 117

6 Strategies and Tools That We Can Use to Help Students Create Global Connections 148

Meet the Author

Rachelle Dené Poth is a Spanish and STEAM teacher at Riverview Junior Senior High School in Oakmont, PA. She is also an attorney and consultant. An ISTE-certified educator, Rachelle is the former president of the ISTE Teacher Education Network, the 2019 recipient of the Making IT Happen Award, and received three Presidential Gold Awards for Volunteer Service to education. She frequently presents at conferences including ASCD, CUE, FETC, ISTE, and TCEA. Her publications include In Other Words: Quotes that Push Our Thinking, Chart a New Course: A Guide to Teaching Essential Skills for Tomorrow's World, The Future Is Now: Looking Back to Move Ahead, True Story Lessons That One Kid Taught Us, and Unconventional Ways to Thrive in EDU. She is a blogger for Getting Smart and several other publications. You can follow her on Twitter and Instagram at @Rdene915 and visit her website at https://sites.google.com/view/rachelledenepoth/about-me.

Introduction

It has been an interesting time for educators. The 2020–21 school year was constantly evolving and pushing us all to embrace new ideas, learn new technologies, face challenges and be flexible in our methods. We had an opportunity to try new ideas, to take some risks with different digital tools and teaching methods as we considered how to plan lessons for our students. Educators around the world spent time looking for the best ways to deliver instruction and for many, this might have been the first time bringing digital tools into their classroom.

It took some time to adjust to all that goes into teaching online. There have been adjustments needed in the devices and equipment we use in our classrooms. My workspace expanded to having two computers, a computer stand or two, an iPad, a microphone, a document camera and a ring light so that my students could actually see me. Beyond the tech adjustments, it was a challenge to figure out a workflow. Moving from fully virtual to hybrid, teaching students in-person and at home simultaneously, took time to adjust. It became clear that we do so many different tasks in our physical classroom space, but it takes a lot longer in the virtual and hybrid environment. It is a process that requires ongoing reflection and iteration. Developing a routine that helps us to minimize a loss of instructional time as we shift between activities is key. Whereas before, we could carry out many tasks and be quite flexible with all students in the

DOI: 10.4324/9781003137665-1

classroom, it now requires more planning and quick thinking in case our plans or technology don't work as we hoped.

Teaching in the virtual space definitely has its benefits. It increases our awareness of the power of technology for connecting our classrooms with resources and people from around the world. But it can be a lot to balance, especially when it comes to technology and deciding what tools to use. We must make sure that all students can participate so they have the most meaningful learning experiences possible while also acknowledging that we have not been in a typical learning situation.

We need to prepare ourselves as best we can for any type of learning environment, whether we suddenly have to make a shift or instead we choose to create more blended learning experiences for our students. Having strategies and tools that we can rely on regardless of our learning space will enable us to keep the learning going and provide consistent support and access to the resources our students need. Throughout school closures and in regular school years, I worry about the students who perhaps are nervous about asking questions or don't have access to their teacher or class materials beyond the class period. Students must feel comfortable in their learning space and be able to seek help and find resources whenever they need them. Technology enables us to provide so much more for our students when we are intentional about the tools we choose.

While we know there are endless benefits to using technology to enhance learning by bringing in possibilities for blended learning, differentiation, facilitating global collaborations and preparing students with future-ready skills, we must be intentional as we plan authentic and meaningful ways for our students to build their presence in the virtual space. We must stay clear on our true purpose for trying a different teaching method and implementing a different or new digital tool. With access to more resources than ever before, it affords us with possibilities to open the world as a classroom for our students and for meeting their different learning styles and interests.

As educators, we are surrounded by technology and have access to more resources and potential for collaboration and using authentic and innovative learning tools and methods with our students. Because we have so much available, it can be challenging to know where to begin. I propose that we ask ourselves this question: What types of learning opportunities do we *need*? The right response is that we need authentic, meaningful and purposeful learning experiences that help us to promote student engagement and increase student motivation for learning. We know how important it is that we create a supportive learning environment, whether that be in the physical or virtual space, and this environment must include the right components to promote more social learning and foster connectedness with the content being taught.

When I am asked where to begin with bringing technology into the learning environment, I believe that first, it is critical that we set up a consistent way to communicate with our students and for them to be able to find support when they need it. Whether we decide on a messaging app, build a class website or have something like Google Classroom or Microsoft Teams, these options give us a consistent space to better communicate and provide for all students. Beyond facilitating better communication, we need to invest time into finding versatile tools that enable students to create, collaborate and connect with peers. Having these capabilities will make a difference for students in many essential areas of their growth.

When I started to bring technology and try new teaching methods into my classroom, it was to resolve a disconnect that I noticed between my students, me and having access to our class materials. The first consistent space I created online was through Edmodo (www.edmodo.com). As a result of that space, I was easily able to connect with each student and address any concerns they had outside of the classroom. Students started to collaborate more, developing their interpersonal skills in the virtual space, which led to more positive peer interactions in the classroom and the development of (SEL) social and emotional learning skills. Students developed more confidence speaking in class, there was an improvement in accountability, students knew when assignments were due and what they had missed in class and they even started to create their own ways to use Edmodo. Leveraging Edmodo provided a lot for what I could make available to my students to help them build language skills in a comfortable space.

Beyond using Edmodo, however, it was initially a challenge for me to break away from the typical activities and class materials that I was accustomed to using in my classroom over the years. I focused on student engagement and building relationships with students to better understand their interests and needs. In doing this, it pushed me to look for ways to better assess students and provide more productive opportunities to practice. We have to create learning experiences where students must create and answers are not easily found through a simple Google search.

As language teachers, we have been battling the use of online translators, and there are even websites that provide students with online answer keys to our language textbooks and workbooks, which makes those activities that have proven to be helpful for students less reliable as ways to assess their learning or provide practice for them. Like all teachers, we face the possibility of students copying the homework assignments, which of course further limits their potential for building skills in the classroom. With these challenges, whether in our classrooms or virtual learning environment, it forces us to think carefully about the tasks we are asking our students to do. I struggled during the past school year to find ways to help my students build their skills without relying on outside resources. Offering support, explaining to students how these translators or other online answer keys not only are inaccurate, but the use of them actually negatively impacts student learning even more. I tried some different digital tools to create a variety of learning activities, hoping that students would feel more confident in taking risks on their own and avoid those other materials. I started to see improvements, and knew I needed to keep trying new ideas.

As educators, we must be willing to take some risks and bring in new methods and tools into our classrooms. We have to make sure that we are connected with other educators and share experiences, successes and failures so that we can become better together as we move forward. We also must remember that when it comes to technology, we can't assume that students know how to use the different tools that we are using, so we must show them and provide support for them as they build their skills. It is frustrating when students turn in work that has been completed using a translator or when they perhaps take answers from an answer key. We need to show them how it can negatively impact their learning potential.

Students have such a fear of making mistakes that it leads them to seek out these answers or translators. Having something that is more than likely correct, is safer than making a mistake in front of others. But we must model for them that making mistakes is how we learn. Many times I have been asked questions to which I did not know the answers. As a world language teacher, I have always felt that it is expected that I know all of the words in the languages that I speak. Of course I do not. It would be awesome if I did, but also I think it is highly impossible. There are so many words in the English language that I do not know and will not ever learn. However, when asked a question, admitting that we do not know the answer can be uncomfortable, especially in the early years of teaching. But no matter where you are in your career, that fear of not knowing an answer might be difficult to handle. It can take some time to realize that it's okay to turn to students for answers to questions. I think this is a good model for our students to show them that it's okay to not know the answer. It's okay to ask others for help. To do this, to truly be comfortable enough to show vulnerability, we have to build and foster supportive relationships in our classrooms. We must focus first on creating the right space for learning to happen and choices that help students to build the right skills for their future.

I came across the Future of Jobs Report of 2018 (*http://www3.weforum.org/docs/WEF_Future_of_Jobs_2018.pdf*), which was shared by The World Economic Forum. A list of the growing skills for 2022 was included in the report and some of the skills in the top ten were: active learning strategies, creativity, critical thinking and complex problem solving, innovation, leadership and emotional intelligence. Think about your own classroom and consider the learning experiences that you could provide for students that would enable them to build these skills while building skills in the target language.

Whenever I think about options for my classroom, I always focus first on how my choices will help students to develop vital skills needed as we navigate the new look of education. As educators, we must help our students to develop the skills that they will need to be successful in the future. But these are also skills that our students need now. During this time, we have to be even more innovative with how we continue teaching our students and finding the right tools to use. Educators must embrace innovation and sometimes the word "innovative" can seem overwhelming or unclear or cause us to keep ourselves safer using the traditional ways we have been teaching. But as educators, we must be willing to take more risks – especially now when we have the chance to try new things and think about more changes that we can make. Education is changing, and we have to stay ahead of those changes. We will bring about some potentially needed and maybe long overdue changes in our own practice and in the look of school itself. We have difficult decisions to make in the work that we do, and we must always be willing to step in and do what is right, not what is easy. And that means being innovative and creating new and different experiences for our students. Even if it means we try and fail. There is learning and growing in failure. Everything in life prepares us for something.

My hope is that through this book you will gain a lot of new ideas and also realize that we all experienced a lot of the same challenges in our classrooms. As we have learned to adjust to the transitions between in-person, hybrid and fully remote instruction, we are all learning as we go. The most important actions that we can take are to be open to new ideas, to stay flexible in our practice, to make sure that we connect with other educators and, most importantly, that we build relationships and continue to seek feedback from our students.

1

Building Relationships and Future-Ready Skills/Designing Our Classroom Space

Chapter Summary

The chapter will focus on the importance of social-emotional learning (SEL) and its significance in the digital environment. As educators, to do the best for our students, we need to be able to identify personal strengths and weaknesses in our teaching practice and reflect so that we can best provide for our students. In our classrooms, we need to help our students to develop these same skills by providing opportunities for them to build their own metacognitive practices and develop skills that are transferable beyond high school. Ideas for helping students to collaborate, to promote student agency, and build essential SEL skills will be shared in this chapter and be applicable to in-person and virtual learning, with quick ideas to get started and some educator vignettes for additional examples.

What to expect in this chapter:

- Ideas to help students build peer relationships
- Ways to engage students in more interactive learning
- Tools and methods that promote collaboration and students as creators of content

DOI: 10.4324/9781003137665-2

At the end of the 2019–20 school year, many of the conversations happening in education were focused on how to best provide for students in virtual learning environments and promote Social-Emotional Learning (SEL) as we transitioned and planned forward. As we plan for the future, we should continue to ask ourselves how we might make those transitions from in our classroom spaces to virtual learning. Also, and perhaps more importantly, how can we leverage the tools available to us to provide support for our students, to create spaces for collaboration and relationship building, and to best prepare our students for the future?

In my personal experience, both as a student enrolled in synchronous and asynchronous courses, as well as having to deliver lessons in these formats and provide online learning experiences for my own students, it is notable what a difference developing one's social presence makes in these environments. There is a certain feeling that develops once students enter the physical classroom. Students entering are welcomed, have a familiarity with the environment, a sense of comfort and knowing what to expect in the classroom. We have time to interact with one another and build relationships. In education, regardless of what form the learning space takes, physical or virtual, these same components should be part of each course or class structure.

Even in normal times, it requires planning and preparation on a consistent basis to truly design the best learning experiences and classroom structures that we can. We must always focus on methods and tools that enable us to provide instruction through varying models of in-person, hybrid and virtual learning spaces. It can be overwhelming to know where to start, but we just have to focus on one thing at a time. For myself, I decided that the best way to prepare is to come up with a list of ideas, and in particular, ones that will be beneficial for students regardless of where we are teaching from. At the start of a new school year and consistently throughout the year, we must focus on fostering connections and communication. If we start by creating opportunities for students to build connections with each other, this will provide the right support we need to work throughout the school year and embrace any challenges that may arise. Building community and supporting social-emotional learning (SEL) needs are more important than ever before.

The additional benefit of extending the discussion between students is that we can help them build collaboration and communication skills by leveraging the technology resources available. As we look toward the future, our students will need to be flexible and have a variety of skills to be successful. By creating more opportunities for students to interact in different digital spaces, we can best prepare them for whatever lies ahead.

The content that we teach is important. We should build upon it by providing opportunities for students to develop social-emotional learning skills and learn to communicate and collaborate on a global scale, regardless of the learning "space." The use of technology continues to increase not just in education, but in all areas of life, especially as we experienced the shifts to fully virtual and hybrid learning. We need to be intentional about embedding opportunities for students to develop their SEL skills, which are critical to their personal and future professional growth.

As we saw over the 2020–21 school year, more than 1 billion students, comprising 90% of the world's learners, were impacted by school closures in 2020. With so many students out of classrooms, it has never been more important to provide experiences that will help them to build their SEL skills so they feel more connected to their peers and the content they are learning.

A great resource for learning more about SEL is the Collaborative for Academic, Social and Emotional Learning (CASEL.org). Research shows that by providing opportunities where we can address the five competencies of SEL, we can positively impact and see an increase in student academic performance. The five SEL competencies are self-awareness, self-management, social awareness, responsible decision making and relationship skills. When we are together in the physical classroom space, there are many options for building these skills. While in a virtual learning environment, we need to be intentional about leveraging the right methods and tools to provide these same opportunities. As language educators, beyond the content that we teach, we must infuse activities that will prepare students for their future. Helping students to learn to effectively manage their time, in particular when working on individual projects or collaboratively, is a vital skill. Another important goal is to empower our students to engage in more self-directed learning and be able to understand their needs and manage emotions and stress. Competency in SEL can positively impact the future success of students, whether in college or in the workplace.

By embedding activities into our curriculum and leveraging different technologies, we can address these essential skills while building language competency. I have seen the positive impact on students engaging in activities which help them to build SEL skills, as it is not specific to any grade level or content area. When it comes to student agency, social emotional learning helps students to work through challenges, develop their workflow and be better able to understand their skills and the steps they need to take to grow. Over the years, I've had many students who can feel defeated because they are not able to master the content or understand the various grammatical constructs in the language they are studying. By providing a space where students can collaborate with peers, share experiences and offer feedback and support to one another, we will help students to build confidence in our classrooms!

Creating, Connecting and Growing

We have the options available which will help students engage in more unique ways to learn more than just the content. Some of the possibilities include bringing in methods such as genius hour, project-based learning (PBL) or place-based learning. We should also consider STEAM focused activities, which will offer students the opportunity to drive their learning, develop essential future-ready skills and build content area knowledge. World language teachers have so many opportunities to try these methods and a variety of digital tools in the classroom that can promote more authentic, hands-on learning for our students, connecting them globally.

Over the years, I have used different categories of digital tools and tried a variety of teaching methods and activities, to promote student engagement and offer more personalized learning experiences. There are so many choices available that will promote student creativity and curiosity and that help us to also foster global connections and cultural understanding. You may already be using some of these tools in your classroom and simply might need to make a slight shift, or reconsider some of the other tools and methods you are using, to expand on the purpose and bring in new learning experiences for your students.

Here are two ideas that will increase student engagement and offer more opportunities for students to apply their language skills in a more meaningful way. These options also connect students with learning beyond our school community, helping them to develop social awareness skills and build relationships.

Flipgrid (www.flipgrid.com). We have used Flipgrid for several years and initially started using it for speaking assessments and reflections for project-based learning (PBL). With an option like Flipgrid, students have a comfortable space where they share ideas, engage in conversations with their peers, receive personalized feedback from their teacher and so much more. Flipgrid is a social learning platform that leverages the power of voice and integrates with many other tools we might already be using in our classrooms. For helping students to become globally connected, there are options to find classrooms to collaborate with using the Grid Pals. By searching through thousands of ideas in "Discovery," teachers can explore different topics and add in the speaking assessment for students to complete. We have an opportunity to leverage Flipgrid as a way for students to build empathy, especially when we create classroom connections with students and educators from around the world. It also offers a space for us to check in with our students to ask about how they are doing, talk about school schedules, share traditions and many more possibilities!

Empatico (www.empatico.org). Empatico will help educators to promote more cultural understanding for all students through the activities they provide and the opportunities for connecting classrooms. Empatico focuses on creating global opportunities

FIGURE 1.1 Flipgrid class check-in

primarily for students ages 6 through 11. As language educators, we can explore the different *activities* available for students to learn about topics including culture, folklore, foods and school. Another great feature of what Empatico offers is through their "bite-size lessons," which are beneficial for helping students to build SEL skills while at home and which then carry over into our classrooms.

Through these options and others like them, we provide opportunities for students to explore new ideas while also creating and building essential SEL skills of self-awareness, self-management, social awareness, relationship skills and responsible decision making. By creating opportunities through these tools and focusing on building SEL, we will engage students in learning experiences that will help with building empathy and developing an appreciation for different perspectives and respecting diversity.

Here are some additional ideas from educators who leverage technology and new ideas to build relationships in the classroom. Each of these options benefits us throughout the year and offers students a chance to become more comfortable and confident in the classroom and in speaking in front of their peers.

Kristen Lyon, Spanish Teacher at Middletown High School, Rhode Island

Fliphunts (Vamos de excursión) with Flipgrid! As fun summatives, I created a Fliphunt to incorporate different themes such as travel, the environment, and ecotourism. Students could choose from a variety of prompts. Some of the prompts included My Life As a Sloth, Turbulence on the Plane, Fly Like a Condor, Let's Go Diving, Birdwatching, Take a Hike, and many others. Fliphunts (scavenger hunts using Flipgrid) were a great way to get kids outside and active while we were finishing last year with full remote learning.

Through the capabilities we now have with technology, the opportunities to connect students and ourselves with learning that takes us out of the physical classroom space are incredible. At the start of the school year in a fully virtual environment, I spent a lot of time trying to create the right space for students to be able to interact with me and with each other. To do this meant coming up with ideas for how we could do introductions, how I could share what I hoped they would learn in class, and my goals for our class this year. I also wanted them to know who I am as a teacher and a person. Having tools like Flipgrid that enable us to do all of this and which are accessible for everyone makes a big difference in developing our classroom community.

We can quickly connect our classrooms with students from other schools, and our students can learn from different teachers. Together we can explore new ideas and strategies as students become global citizens and collaborators. These types of learning spaces will help students to better understand and develop essential skills they will need in the future while developing their target language skills. So where or how do we provide these different learning spaces for students?

For many years, I kept myself isolated and did not understand the power of connections. I have learned how much of an impact those connections can make on my own personal and professional development and the even greater impact it has on students. We must start by making sure that we are connected beyond our school community, whether by leveraging social media and different learning networks, attending conferences, reading blogs, listening to podcasts for ideas or picking up educational books on topics that we wish to learn more about.

Fiama Liaudat, Argentine teacher working in a Spanish immersion Kindergarten classroom, public school in Tarboro, North Carolina, USA

One of the first things I did when I knew we had to teach virtually was to start playing with the virtual tools we could access for free. Google Slides is something that I use for literally EVERYTHING. I spent a whole Sunday looking for pictures in PNG format, taking advantage of other teachers' documents and trying to remember all of the details we have in our real classroom, and I tried to re-create them in this virtual space. I think that having a virtual classroom is a great strategy to help students experience a sense of belonging to a group, to their kindergarten, to their teachers. We take care of every detail: letters, numbers, expectations, calendar, cultural corners. Instead of standing up in front of them in our real class, we were using this virtual classroom as our main stage for every single thing we needed to do. And it worked really well for us! Also, we used a lot of Bitmoji, one app that allows you to create your own 3D character. We use it not only to personalize our messages and classroom, but also to send feedback for our kids' activities. When you work in kindergarten, you know that establishing and maintaining relationships with your students is the most important thing, and sometimes the abstract of the virtuality could make it difficult.

We need to stay current and relevant so that we can design the best learning experiences for our students, and that means stepping outside of our comfort zones and trying new things too! Not that we need to be an expert or create everything *for* them; we simply need to get them started and let them design their learning path in the space they decide best fits their interests and needs. To do this, we need to make sure that we first learn about our students and create those spaces for them to learn about each other. Especially when helping students to develop their language skills, we want them to be confident when writing, speaking, reading, and listening in our classroom. We can use the tools and methods to help them build these essential skills.

FIGURE 1.2 "About Me" Buncee with video introduction (*https://app.edu.buncee.com/buncee/be23902151264b74ab9e3dcecbe3bed2*)

1. Communicating and Connecting

An essential first step is for our students and their families to get to know us. There are many ways that we can do this using some of the digital tools and technologies out there. I love using a tool like Flipgrid, where we can introduce ourselves, share ideas, have fun and provide space for students to record their own introduction, so we can get to know them too. Being able to see and hear each other will help with promoting the development of a supportive learning community.

Beyond the video response tools, another favorite in my classroom for many years has been *Buncee* (www.buncee.com), a multi-media creation tool. It is a one-stop shop for educators and students! There are thousands of ready-made templates to choose from that are great for the start of the year, including "Meet the Teacher" or "About Me," and many more for having students share their learning in more authentic ways throughout the year. What I appreciate most about these options is that you are able to record a video or greeting to students, include relevant links and documents even, making it easier to share with students.

Another feature of tools like Buncee and Flipgrid is that they have Immersive Reader which not only promotes accessibility but can also help students to build confidence in their language skills. For students who might be nervous about speaking in Spanish, they can use Immersive Reader to hear native speakers reading

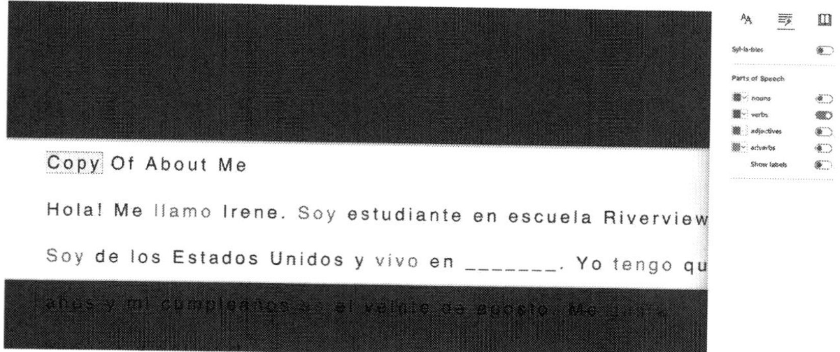

FIGURE 1.3 Immersive Reader in Buncee

Luis Oliveira, ELL and Spanish Teacher, Rhode Island

By far the tool that I use that makes all activities accessible to my ELs is the Immersive Reader. It can be found in so many programs that we use, including our favorites (Flipgrid, Wakelet, Buncee, and within our Teams Learning Environment). The translation features, Read Aloud, and the Picture Dictionary make it possible for all of my language learners to participate in all activities. How much the students use the Immersive Reader depends on their level of English acquisition. The students are given the freedom to use as much or as little as needed depending on their individual needs.

their text as a way to practice and develop their own pronunciation skills. Students in my classes have done this and mentioned how a tool like Flipgrid helps with becoming more comfortable when speaking in Spanish and is a good space to build relationships by engaging in conversations with peers or receiving direct and personalized video feedback from teachers.

As with all digital tools, we have so many possibilities to choose from, but it still comes down to what the particular focus or purpose is. My preference has been to use Buncee because I love creating with it and, more importantly, my students love all the possibilities for using it in Spanish!

Another tool that educators enjoy creating with as well as having students design is *Canva* (www.canva.com), which offers an educator account. They offer lesson plans, schedules, presentation formats, and also have templates for you to use. It is easy to create a page, class brochure, or other graphic format for students to introduce themselves to their peers and you. It is also important that we participate in these activities along with our students so we can build relationships and share the fun in learning with them!

2. Building Community

Something that I haven't done in my classroom for many years and that I personally was not a big fan of was doing ice breakers. It wasn't until many years into my teaching career that I realized the importance of designing activities, whether at the start of the year or throughout the year, for students and myself to build relationships and to get to know each other so that we could truly have a supportive learning community.

It's more than simply participating in a quick game or doing something like "3 truths and a lie" or other types of activities that we create. It has to go beyond basic introductions and focus more on creating opportunities for us to learn more about each individual's unique needs and interests.

While icebreakers may not be a favorite for everyone, there are fun options that we can try in our classroom and that do not take a lot of time to get started with. Some quick ideas include doing something like a "Things I Wish My Teacher Knew," the "Three Truths and a Lie," or "Ten Facts About Me." With any of these three options, technology is not required to get started although there are definitely options available with some of the digital tools like Buncee. And what I think is also important is that teachers must be willing to participate in these activities with students. Take it from someone who didn't believe in the power of building those student-teacher relationships for many years. The value in doing activities like this and investing the time will pay off.

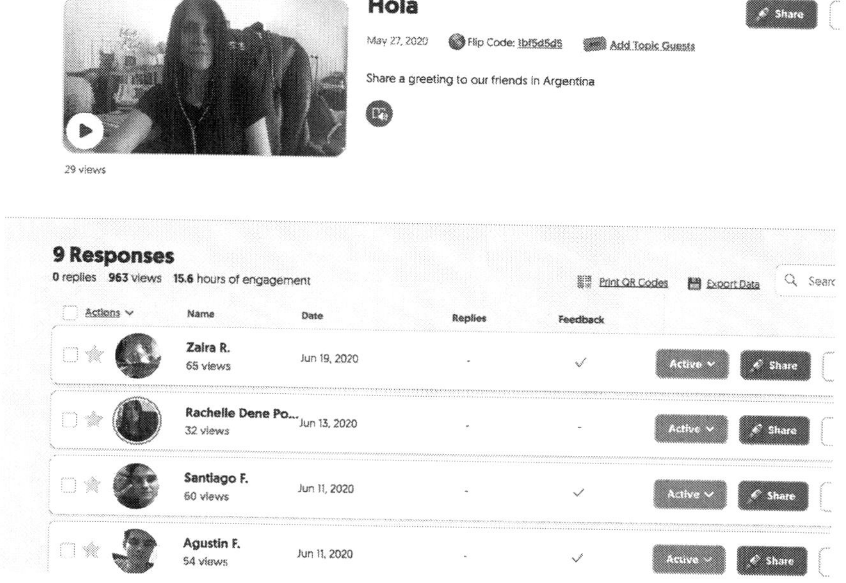

FIGURE 1.4 Flipgrid PBL collaboration with Argentina

> **Fiama Liaudat**
>
> Quick ideas from Fiama for connecting and creating community:
>
> - Share a good morning message with a video made with our Bitmojis to keep the routines of our morning meetings at school.
> - Offer office hours as spaces for our kids to connect with us and share whatever they want with us: a snack, a conversation, a book, some memory. It was another space to continue building that teacher-student relationship.
> - Send notes of gratitude and appreciation to students. For this we use pictures, short videos, and some TikTok sets so they could have fun with it because just sending a text doesn't work in Kindergarten, they don't read yet!

When we truly put ourselves out there and make those connections with our students, help them to see what they have in common with their classmates and build that collaborative and supportive space, we will see how it positively impacts the learning that happens in our classroom every single day. There are also a lot of options for doing these types of ice breaker activities by using some of the different digital tools available. It might be something like having students post responses using Microsoft Teams or using a Padlet where each student creates a post, shares a video or makes a list of their interests that they feel comfortable sharing. We can also use Buncee and Flipgrid for making connections when we can't be in the physical classroom space.

FIGURE 1.5 A virtual Bitmoji classroom by Fiama

3. Creating the Right Spaces

Something that became tremendously popular when schools first closed in March of 2020 was the creation of virtual classroom spaces. Whether using Google Slides or *Slides Mania* (www.slidesmania.com) with Bitmojis or designing one with Buncee, educators wanted to find a way to help students feel as though they were still part of the regular classroom setting. Students were able to visit their virtual classroom to find the class materials and resources they needed and be a part of the class community and space. It helped us to feel like it was a bit more normal. Teachers were able to add in audio or video to create a more engaging virtual classroom environment!

I couldn't wait to dive in and create my own! I chose to create a Buncee virtual classroom where I added in a few slides that made it feel more like our classroom space. It was fun to design the space, adding a whiteboard with a video embedded that I recorded to greet students or give details about our plans for the week. I even had a bookshelf in the classroom where I hyperlinked nine different digital tools that we use most often, so students could be taken directly to each website without having to type anything. There are a lot of possibilities using the audio and video tools in Buncee. We can use them to post a message,

FIGURE 1.6 My Buncee virtual classroom

greet students or explain something and have it be available to them whenever students need it, without worrying about them missing out during class meetings. With not all students having reliable access to devices or Wi-Fi at varying times, it is crucial to provide a space where students can feel connected and find the answers they need. And most importantly, to be able to hear directly from me. Students need to feel connected to us, and having a space like this makes a big difference.

What makes these virtual classrooms unique is that it creates a space for students to access class resources, to feel connected in a classroom space, and it gives teachers a chance to interact with students through the audio and video options available. With Buncee, we can really create an interactive classroom space!

As we move forward, we may continue to find ourselves transitioning to and from our physical classroom space, however we will be better prepared because we have our prior experiences to draw upon. Through the challenges experienced during the school years impacted by the pandemic, we explored and embraced new possibilities for amplifying the learning potential for our students.

Ide Koulbanis, World Cultures and French Teacher, Rhode Island

Technology can help us achieve so much in our personal and professional life. Harnessing the power of technology to foster and build relationships is invaluable.

Case and point – my love for Buncee.

Buncee is an amazing, online creation tool that I use in my World Cultures and French classes. My World Cultures class is a "special" in our middle school, so the fifth graders have it for just one quarter. There is usually lots of "oohing" and "aahing" when my fifth graders first enter the realm of Buncee!

The very first day I usually give them a tour of the platform and show them some design tips and tricks. I usually challenge them to create their first Buncee with a "Guess That Movie" challenge.

More Ideas to Try for Building Language Skills and Relationships

Exploring Our Options

As language educators, we have many options available which will help students engage in more unique ways to learn more than just the content, so we can prepare them for the future. World language

FIGURE 1.7 "Guess That Movie" Buncee

> The first assignment I have them create on their own is a "Get to know you" activity.
>
> I share my Buncee with them by creating a Board to post them on. My Buncee has all the instructions as well as my own example pages so they get to know me too! Using the Buncee Board codes, it is super simple for them to share their Buncees and then be able to see one another's work also. This activity typically takes a couple of class periods, as they need time to work on their own, and then we usually do an all-class share out of their work on the projector.
>
> The beauty of the Buncee Boards is that some of my more shy, introverted students might not want to share out in class, but their peers can still get to know about them by checking out all the Buncees on the Board. I love that they can comment and like one another's Buncees also – another way for them to model being engaged, digital citizens.
>
> This is a great ice breaker and relationship building activity!

teachers have so many opportunities to try these methods and a variety of digital tools in the classroom that can promote more authentic, hands-on learning for our students.

There are many ways we can help students to build relationships in the classroom. Each of these will benefit us throughout the year and give students the chance to become more comfortable and confident in the classroom, especially when speaking in front of their peers. For some quick ideas that don't require a lot of time to get started with, if students meet using Google Meet, Microsoft Teams or Zoom, it is a good idea to check in with students by doing a quick activity. Whether you create a Google Slides presentation and post one slide each day and ask students to respond in the chat using an emoji or number based on the images you share or explore some of the free presentations available through Slides Mania, there are a lot of choices for us that help us to do a quick status check on our students.

Some of my favorite ways that are easy to do include creating a quick Google form that have some required questions but also some that are optional for students which ask about how they're feeling, if they are experiencing any challenges with the hybrid or virtual learning or the content and if there's anything that I can help them with. Of course, these questions are all written in the target language, and students are encouraged to respond in Spanish where applicable. It also provides a good review of some of the basic verbs for expressing one's feelings or describing activities and in a safe space where I can better understand my students' needs and provide support for them.

There are also days where I might want a quick game of Quizizz or a Kahoot! to ask similar questions or create a Flipgrid prompt or a Buncee presentation to talk to my students and ask for their feedback and for them to check in with me. There are many possibilities whether we use the technology available to us or based on our observations or interactions in the classroom. However, with us not being in our traditional classroom space, it is important to have a range of possibilities that we can choose from, that will work for our students and will provide us with the information that we need to best support them.

Beyond our own classroom community, we can quickly connect our classrooms with students and teachers from around the world. Together we can explore new ideas and strategies and students can become globally connected citizens. These types of learning spaces will help

Jimena Licitra, languages teacher at Colegio Miramadrid in Madrid, Spain

SEL is super important for students, much more than they tell us. During COVID-19, I decided to use Pear Deck to check in and see how my students were doing. I included a question in German for them to answer and I got many responses thanking me for worrying about them. It was a very special moment and connection between us.

Students responded with kind messages and found the tool very easy to use. In fact, now I use Pear Deck much more because they ask me to!

students to better understand and develop essential skills they will need in the future while developing their language skills in more meaningful ways. So where or how do we provide these different learning spaces for students? Here are some examples to explore!

*****

More Ideas to Try for Building Language Skills and Relationships

There have been a lot of ideas, strategies and tools shared in this chapter. It is always helpful to have a go-to list of possible tools to explore with one or two ideas of how to use each of those tools. Here are seven to try for a quick start to promote SEL skills and help students to build language skills confidently in and out of the classroom.

With each of these options, there are many other ways to use these tools in our language classrooms, whether in person, hybrid or fully virtual. The idea is to find one or two tools that enable us to do a lot in our classrooms and that promote student choice and voice in learning.

> **Kristen Lyon**
>
> In my Spanish classes, we've had a "Bring your pet to school day." While digital, students bring their pets to class and we use it to practice introductions, descriptive adjectives, and the verb *gustar*. At the end of class discussion, students can post a picture of their pet in the chat. After class, students go back and post comments describing what they learned about each other's furry family members.
>
> Use Microsoft Teams chat, emojis and GIFs to post birthday messages or congratulations for various achievements. We used emojis as we learned food vocabulary in Spanish. I would name a food and kids would post an emoji expressing their opinions, and in reverse, I would post an emoji and they would write the food that matched that feeling.

1. Buncee: Buncee is the "one stop shop" tool that educators and students need for creating a multimedia presentation full of animations, emojis, stickers, 3D objects, 360 images, audio

and video and more. Start by exploring the ready-made templates available to create an "About Me" or a "Things I Wish My Teacher Knew," or find another relevant topic. Create your own and then use a Buncee Board to have students share theirs with classmates. Encourage students to record audio or video in their Buncee so that we can all get to see and hear each other and also practice language speaking skills. A great way to start building relationships with our students and even globally connecting!

2. Flipgrid: Mentioned several times by educators who shared in this chapter, there are many ways to use Flipgrid in our language classroom. Whether we create our own prompts for students or we select from some of the topics already available in the discussion library, we can use Flipgrid for building language skills, confidence and promoting the development of SEL skills too! Creating a Fliphunt can be used in any learning environment, and in addition to helping students to develop reading, writing, listening and speaking skills in the target language, they will build collaboration and creativity skills too.
3. Kahoot! (www.kahoot.com) A game-based learning tool that is a fantastic option for providing some practice in class, for assessments or even Kahoot! Challenges that are student paced. Depending on the age of your students, another idea that can be fun is to have students create their own game of Kahoot! to use for classmates to get to know each other or perhaps for you to create an "About Me" game after introducing yourself to your students. Also explore Kahoot! as a way to check-in with students and gather feedback about how students are doing not only academically but in relation to wellbeing.
4. Nearpod: (www.nearpod.com) You will learn many ways to use Nearpod in your language classes throughout the year. However, when it comes to SEL, there are two ways that I enjoy using Nearpod to promote SEL. First, I like to create a quick launch, which is one activity that I can use to have students do a quick check-in, to see how they are

doing and how they feel about their progress. The other way that I enjoy using Nearpod is taking some of the SEL-focused lessons and adding in images, videos or VR trips to Spanish-speaking locations. These lessons promote discussion in our class and help students become more socially aware as they explore and make comparisons with their own communities and perspectives. It also helps students to develop empathy as they learn about different communities.

5. Padlet: (www.padlet.com) Padlet is a virtual wall that promotes collaboration, can be used for class discussions, curating resources for a class project, brainstorming or even scavenger hunts. Talk about having fun with language learning! Asking students to find objects on a scavenger hunt list and post them to the Padlet is collaborative learning and definitely authentic. Or start by simply asking students to post a few facts about themselves or do a "Three Truths and a Lie" game. It can be a fun way to get to know each other, especially if we are not in the same physical classroom space. Beyond our own classroom community, consider using Padlet for global collaborations too.
6. Synth: (www.gosynth.com) A free option that has a lot of possibilities is using Synth, a podcasting tool. I have used it for recording listening comprehension activities or explaining a concept for class and also for doing student check-ins. Why not have students create their own language podcast where they can discuss a topic or work with classmates to interview a "special guest"? We can include some performance-based assessments using a tool like Synth and give students a chance to track their growth over time as they record additional podcast episodes. Using this type of platform can be a different way to engage students in a discussion and promote the building of relationships.
7. Zigazoo: Zigazoo is similar to Instagram with the feel of TikTok, and my students enjoy creating 30-second Zigazoo videos in response to a prompt. You can choose

from many Zigazoo educator channels that provide daily prompts and then have your students respond in Spanish. It is another fun option to use for speaking assessments, as a way to do introductions for classmates or as a different way to check in with students. Great for SEL as students get to learn about their classmates and also, depending on the prompts that you select, expand their cultural and global awareness.

We can choose from some of the hands-on learning activities, create spaces for students to engage in conversations and collaborative work or help them to build SEL skills by using a variety of the game-based learning tools that promote collaboration and communication and definitely critical thinking. Students always enjoy when I bring a new game or interactive lesson tool into the classroom because it gives them a different way to practice the content and, in many cases, facilitates additional interactions with classmates, even if not in the same physical space. A favorite this year has been Blooket (www.blooket.com), which will be shared in greater detail in a later chapter. However, when it comes to SEL, using tools like Blooket or Gimkit, for example, where students can work with the game mechanics, have conversations with each other whether in or out of the classroom and engage in more social learning goes a long way to helping them to feel more connected in the classroom. Of course, it also helps them to build self-awareness as they learn to assess their own strengths and set new goals for what they need to work on.

There are so many choices out there, and these are just a few to try. You will hear about these tools throughout the book as they provide a lot of possibilities for educators and can be used to help students to build confidence in language learning while promoting the development of skills essential for the future.

Student in Spanish III, Grade 11

What I love about some of the different games is that they ease you into learning. When I play, I am initially focused more on winning than trying to learn, therefore learning happens naturally and isn't forced. I improve my language skills as I continue to focus more on being correct and analyzing the choices!

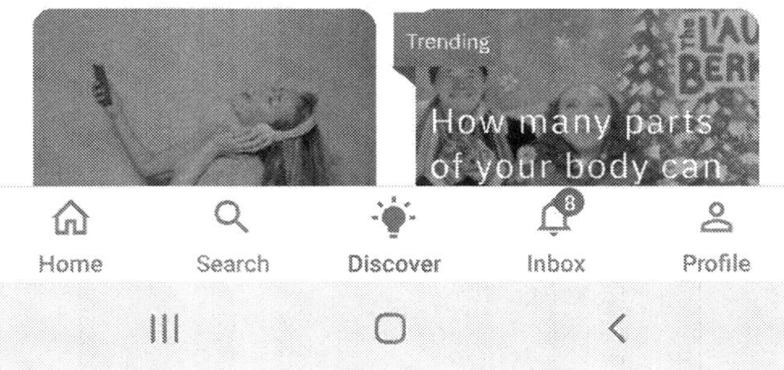

FIGURE 1.8 Options available in Zigazoo app

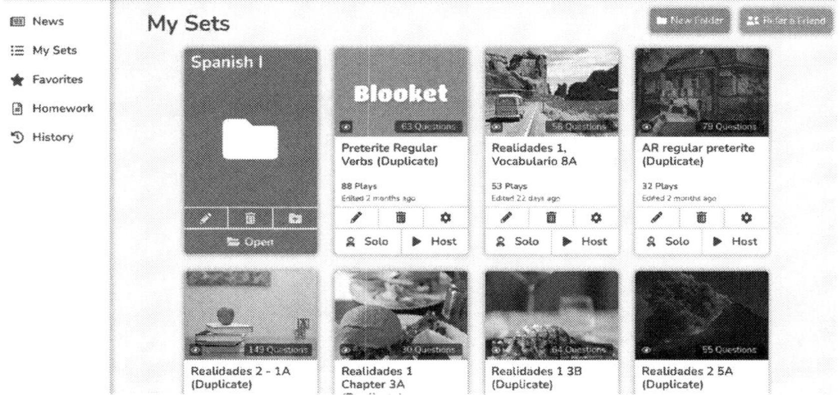

FIGURE 1.9 Dashboard of Blooket, showing sets and folders created

As we consider the tools that we want to use in our classroom, we must focus on the underlying purpose behind choosing a certain tool or a method. As language educators, when we bring in different options that promote student use of the target language, starting from the first day of our classes, whether in person or virtually, we work on building confidence and comfort of students in our learning space. We will create a space to foster collaboration, increase student motivation for learning, and help students to feel better supported during their language learning journey.

2

Low Tech, High Tech, No Tech

Learning for All

Chapter Summary

In this chapter, you will learn many ideas for promoting more movement in the classroom, to accommodate accessibility and range of devices and resources available to educators and students. Explore ideas that will engage students through different activities and methods of instruction using some tech or no tech at all. Try different teaching strategies which involve music and games that get students more actively involved in learning. While it can feel like a challenge to change over from the traditional classroom lecture model or prior methods we have used, there are easy ways to transition to a more active, engaging space.

What to expect in this chapter:

- Ideas for interactive learning for hybrid and online learning
- Tools to promote student choice and confidence in learning
- How to create learning stations

Over the years there were a lot of times that I thought I wasn't doing enough in my classroom. I would hear about different teaching methods or read about an acronym used in education and honestly

DOI: 10.4324/9781003137665-3

didn't have a clue about what they were or how to get started. But what I found many of those times is that I was in fact doing some of those things, I just didn't attach a specific name to them. For example, app smashing, differentiation, personalized learning and SEL. I had already been making some changes to "the way I had always done things" by bringing in digital tools, finding language websites and having students choose which activities to complete and guiding them along as needed. I also started to combine different digital tools and have students create something as an end product but didn't realize that what I was doing was "app smashing." The point is that sometimes our strategies and the tools that we use come to us not because of something that we've read but because we developed our own ideas over time or have come across a digital tool. We've either tried other strategies and tools that became our traditional choices or maybe taught the same way we were taught, like in my own case, but we've all made improvements and changes in our practice over time that have led to better results for our students.

We can make choices that have the greatest impact by giving students more of an opportunity to be active in language learning, to move them from simply being the consumers and passive learners to becoming the creators and leaders in the classroom. We need to get them up and moving as much as possible, and whether that's in the physical space and moving around the room or if it's in the virtual space and they are shifting between different activities set up for them online, we have a lot of possibilities to choose from.

I consider the types of strategies and digital tools that I use each school year and reflect regularly. In teaching Spanish levels I through IV, there are some practices and tools that have remained a constant choice in my classes because of all of the options and new ways that I figure out how to use them. Sometimes I learn new ideas from my students. There are new tools that we try each year that get added into my regular "toolkit" because of the benefits that I notice for students and maybe more importantly, their response to using them.

The tools that stay in my toolkit each year are there because of the versatility they offer, the new ways that we discover they can be used to build language retention and because they provide an abundance of choice for student learning. It is not uncommon for me to start each year with students in Spanish 1 by having them create an "About me" presentation using a specific digital tool like Buncee and in the upper levels of Spanish, giving choices of the more interactive platforms to have students create and lead in the classroom. I like to provide many different types of learning activities for students because it gives them the opportunity to engage with the content using a variety of modalities. It also promotes a more personalized learning experience for students.

When so many options are available, where should we begin? What I recommend is what I have put into my own practice. When we try some new methods or I use different digital tools with my instruction, I reflect on a few guiding questions:

1. What did the digital tool or method help me to do better as a teacher?
2. Did it promote student engagement or positively impact the students' learning potential?
3. Was I able to empower students through more authentic and personalized learning opportunities as a result?

In the 2020–21 school year, I also evaluated the methods and tools that were helpful as we transitioned through school closures and in-person, hybrid and fully virtual learning environments. It's important that we have a variety of options available to us, especially if we find that we do need to make those transitions or simply because we want to leverage more impactful digital options with our students.

In addition to these guiding questions and considerations, we must make sure that all students have the access to the technologies that we are using or that we offer multiple alternatives in case students don't have access to the tools they need. There are so many benefits to bringing technology in. Beyond giving students a more personalized learning experience and being able to differentiate our instruction, we are better able to provide students with authentic, meaningful and timely feedback. Providing this is critical for learning, and it also promotes communication and collaboration between classmates.

To get started, I recommend that you first take a look at some versatile tools that can help us do a lot of different tasks in our classrooms, especially when it comes to assessments for learning. Whether you want students to simply take some of the vocabulary or verbs and create with the language each digital tools offers versatile choices. These digital tools can even be good for having students create and lead their own lessons for a more personalized and student-driven way to demonstrate learning.

Here are some ideas that have worked well in my class for assessing students and promoting student choice and voice in the classroom.

1. I talk about Buncee (www.buncee.com) a lot because it has been a favorite for my students for several years and it offers what I have referred to as a "one stop shop" for creating multimedia and interactive presentations. It is easy to get started with and for teachers, there are thousands of templates available that can be used in our language classrooms. The Ideas Lab is where teachers can find thousands of lesson ideas for use in the classroom that can be adaptable to our specific target language needs. We can also share our own ideas to be added to the Ideas Lab for other educators. What I love is when we find tools that are great for teachers and students to be the creators, whether for creating a lesson or having students respond to a prompt and create a visual representation of their learning.

A few years ago, one of my students completed her summer assignment by creating a verb lesson using Buncee. In my school, teachers assign summer activities for students to work on as preparation for the next school year. I have shifted from designing the review activities myself and instead have students create a review lesson we can use at the start of the new school year. One year, one of my students came in and said that she had her Buncee. At first I was not sure what she meant. What she had done was create a lesson on regular verb conjugations using Buncee. She conjugated the verbs, added in some examples and a video into the presentation and she led the class through the lesson. It was a great experience for her to create the lesson, and it has become a resource for me as a teacher to use each year. It's something that I can share with

FIGURE 2.1 Student-created lesson with Buncee

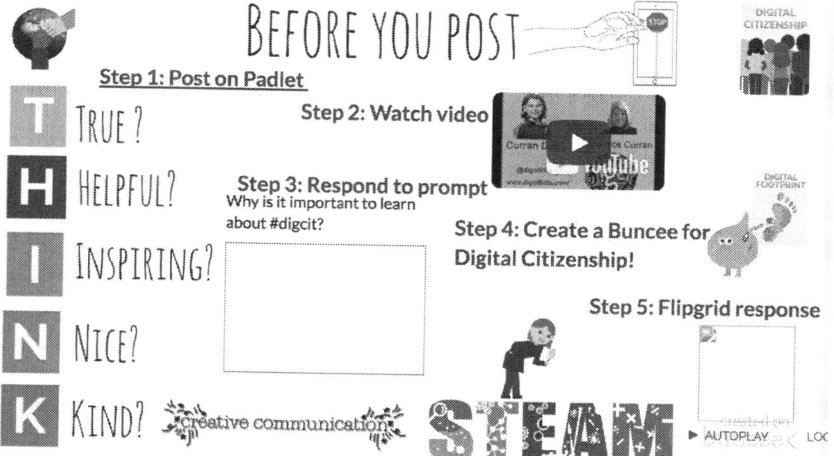

FIGURE 2.2 First interactive lesson created with Buncee

students who are looking for additional support as they learn how to conjugate verbs, in this case. It gives students a very meaningful purpose for creating and sharing their learning with classmates.

As I mentioned earlier, Buncee also has Immersive Reader, which increases accessibility for all students and provides more robust ways to learn, especially for language learners. The benefit of Immersive Reader in the digital tools we use is that it enables our class materials and student projects to be shared with classrooms around the world.

2. Edpuzzle. Years ago, I had been taking time in class to show instructional videos and realized that I should find a better way to maximize our class time together. I shifted to having students watch videos outside of class and gave "flipped learning" methods a try. However, what I found was that not all students were actually watching the video the same as they would if we were together in the classroom. In the classroom, it was more interactive, but we still lost time by watching the video. I needed to find a way to keep students accountable while also giving them more of an interactive experience like they would have if they were in our classroom. There were a few tools that I explored including Playposit and Edpuzzle. I started using Edpuzzle because I could create an interactive video lesson from a video that I made or one found on YouTube and I could get started with it quickly.

Using Edpuzzle is a great option whether in our classrooms or working with remote instruction. Getting started with Edpuzzle is easy, especially since there are video lessons available to choose from that you can edit to make your own. With each video, you can add multiple choice questions, notes or open-ended responses for students to work through as they watch video and process the information at their own pace. If you prefer creating your own instructional videos, you can then upload them and add questions. It is a quick process to even find a YouTube video and create a short video lesson for students. When I have asked my students for feedback, they have shared that they enjoy using the app to complete the lessons on their phone and being able to think through more closely. As a teacher, it is helpful to be able to track their individual progress and provide direct feedback quickly. Everything appears in your teacher dashboard and you can see student progress over time. For asynchronous class days, using Edpuzzle is a great option for creating some student-paced activities. It gives us data that we can use to better plan our

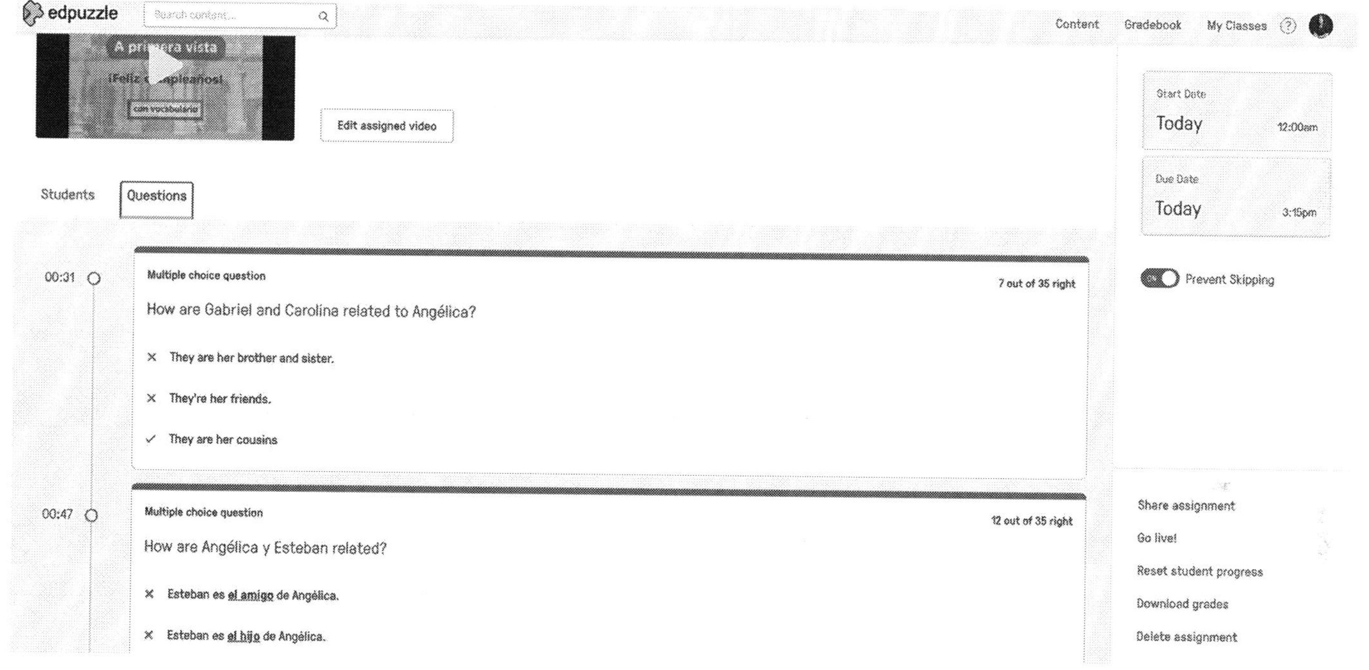

FIGURE 2.3 Layout of Edpuzzle lesson and options

lessons and to provide feedback to students, and it also enables students to complete it at a time that works for them.

3. Flipgrid started as simply a video response tool and has evolved into a social learning platform. Students and educators can record a video response and video prompts can include additional content such as Buncee presentations, Nearpod lessons or Newsela or Wonderopolis articles. For remote teaching last year, Flipgrid provided an easy way to do screen recordings. There are many other tools out there, but with Flipgrid, a recording is free and can be up to ten minutes. Using Flipgrid provides a comfortable and fun way for students to exchange ideas about what they are learning, as a way to reflect or provide feedback to classmates or to explore topics in the discovery library to build speaking skills. We have also used it to connect globally with students from Argentina and Spain, which also makes it helpful for developing the core competencies of SEL. As many other tools out there, it is easy to get started by searching from more than 10,000 ready-to-launch topics that can quickly be adapted for use in the language classroom.

Using some of the resources available within the Flipgrid Discovery Library, we can also bring in STEM content and more, for our students to apply their language skills. As a language teacher, I started to teach a course in STEAM and focused on Spanish and French culture for the arts. It provided me with new ideas for my Spanish classes, including doing problem- and

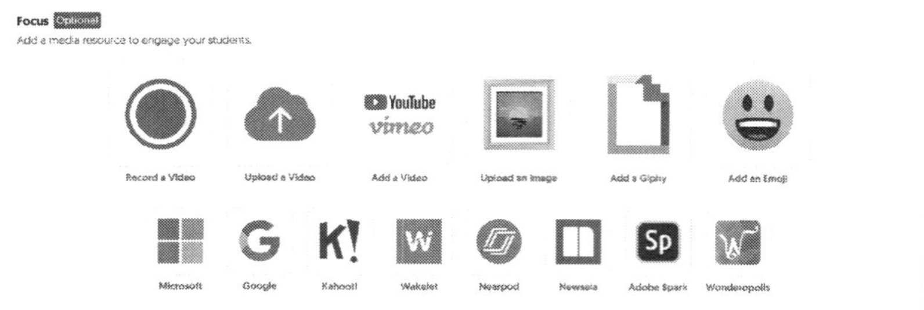

FIGURE 2.4 Options to add to a Flipgrid topic

project-based learning. During our PBL work, students made connections with peers in Argentina and using Flipgrid, could ask specific questions, learn about home and school life through the videos that students shared and feel more connected.

4. Gimkit is one of many game-based learning tools that has been a favorite with my students each year. As with other similar tools, it gives students the opportunity to have more personalized learning experiences. It offers something different than the other digital tools because it promotes increased content retention through the repetitive questions that are asked and multiple ways it can be played in or out of the classroom. A fun feature is the new Gimkit draw, talk about interactive and fun learning. Another benefit is that we can help students to build SEL skills through the game as they play on teams or simply engage in collaboration with classmates. They have fun building their language skills!

Getting started is easy: you can search the pre-made kits or upload your own vocabulary to create a game fast. The data that is available after playing helps us to better plan for our students and provide additional differentiation in our lessons as needed. We can get a general overview to see how the class did, looking at the specific number of responses that were correct and incorrect for each question, or we can look at each student's performance. There are multiple game modes to choose from which increase student engagement. What teachers can appreciate about all of these game options, especially those that have students working on teams, is that they can help students to become better at communicating as they develop their skills. It provides them with additional opportunities to practice speaking in the target language while they are engaged in the game and practicing the content that they are learning. It also helps them to gain additional practice with their everyday conversational speech. They can negotiate meaning as they exchange information with their peers, and I can also use it as an opportunity to review additional vocabulary by the questions that I ask them. For preparing to use in the classroom, Gimkit does not require that questions be projected onto one screen for

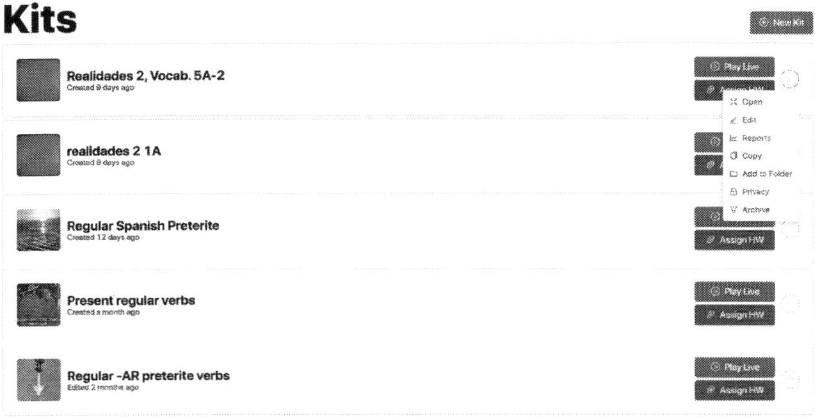

FIGURE 2.5 Gimkit dashboard showing "kits" and options for each

students to see, which helps with virtual learning environments. It also offers the option for games to be assigned for student paced as practice, which students always enjoy!

5. *Formative* (www.goformative.com) is a versatile tool for use in creating digital formative assessments and which has proven to be quite beneficial, especially during the past school year with virtual and hybrid learning. I struggled with finding options for assessing students that would either fully deter or limit the tendency to use translators or other online resources. Without being together in the same classroom space, it becomes challenging to create assessments that will provide a clear picture of individual student progress and give us access to data that we can act upon quickly.

   Finding a tool that offers multiple ways for students to show learning and that can be used in any environment can be a challenge. With Formative, interactive lessons can be created quickly and include open-ended, multiple choice, resequencing, a drawing space and more.

Ide Koulbanis

My students LOVE all the different Gimkit modes and we love to change it up. One particular class is super competitive and loves to challenge me in Boss Mode! It is me playing against all of them and they get so excited!

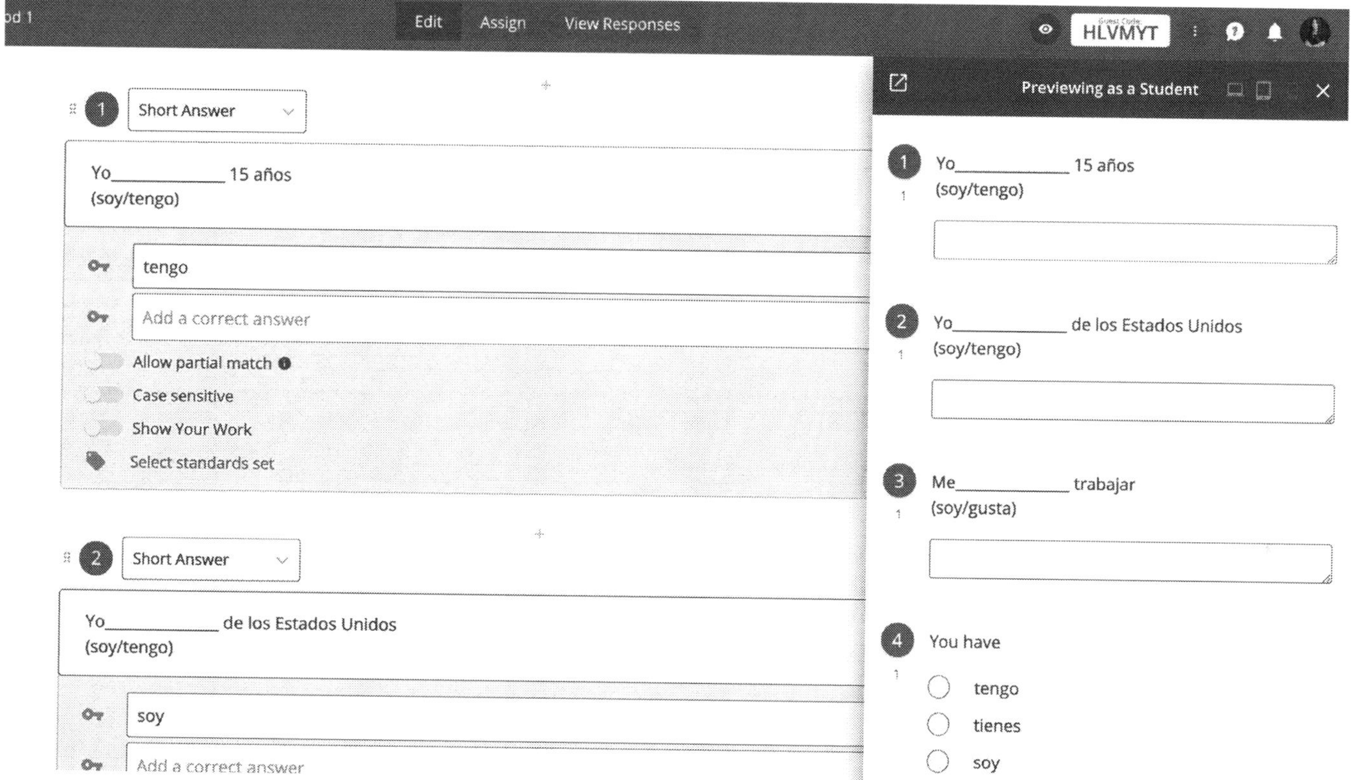

FIGURE 2.6 Creating and previewing a Formative lesson

> For teachers looking for a new tool, I recommend finding one that offers a lot of possibilities for students to be more involved in the lesson and that we can use to include a variety of tasks and content to support students. During virtual and hybrid learning, I felt confident that Formative would prove to be a good choice for students to show their learning progress and enable me to provide them with timely and meaningful feedback.

As with the other tools mentioned, there are many "Formatives" already available in the library for immediate use in your classroom. These Formatives can also be edited to meet your specific assessment needs, especially because of the variety of question types and activities or multimedia resources that can be included. If your school uses Google Classroom, you can assign the Formatives directly to your students. You can also create a class within Formative or provide students with a code.

There are several options which help to promote academic integrity, including scrambling the question order, not allowing edits, setting a timer and not allowing responses or scores to be viewed after submission. Teachers can select from different question types including drawing, matching, multiple choice, resequencing, short response, audio and more, as well as uploading content and videos into the Formative. Providing feedback to students is streamlined through the use of the comment feature that sends your feedback directly to students. I relied on this heavily during our remote instruction as it gave me the best way that I could come up with to assess students, to be able to see their progress in real time and have the data so that I could provide them with actionable feedback.

6. Nearpod (www.nearpod.com) A few years ago I was introduced to Nearpod and first used it with my Spanish 3 class to take them on a virtual trip to South America. For years I had been asking students to "imagine" what it would be like to go to the places we learned about or using videos on YouTube to show them what it looked like, however these weren't truly immersive experiences.

My students were more engaged in the Nearpod lesson because they could more closely explore the places we had been reading about. For anyone not familiar with it, Nearpod is a multimedia, interactive presentation tool that enables teachers to design engaging lessons full of content such as 3D objects, virtual trips, videos and more. Nearpod offers thousands of ready-made lessons for different content areas and grade levels. It also has English learner lessons and a variety of lesson packages focused on grammar and culture topics for French and Spanish, and more are always being added. There are so many lessons to choose from, which helps as we look for new ideas but may not have a lot of extra time to invest. What makes it so beneficial is that you can get started with a lesson without much time at all by using one of the options available in the library and quickly choosing from the different content and activities to include.

Designing lessons does not take much time to get started and lessons can include audio and video, drawings, matching pairs, polls, quizzes and additional content-focused, content area-specific tools. A favorite activity is the Time to Climb game. Nearpod lessons can be done live in class or student paced. Another option is having students create their own Nearpod lesson, depending on their age. I did this with my juniors and seniors in Spanish III and IV for review lessons and for project-based learning. Students enjoyed the opportunity to create something they could use to do a presentation in class that shifted some of the focus away from them and more to a class experience.

Especially helpful in hybrid or distance learning, lessons delivered through Nearpod have been great options for immersing students in interactive learning experiences. Nearpod also has the Immersive Reader, which again helps promote accessibility, especially for students building their language skills and for helping students to become more confident in speaking in the target language. We can choose from lessons that are available and have students take advantage of the Immersive Reader

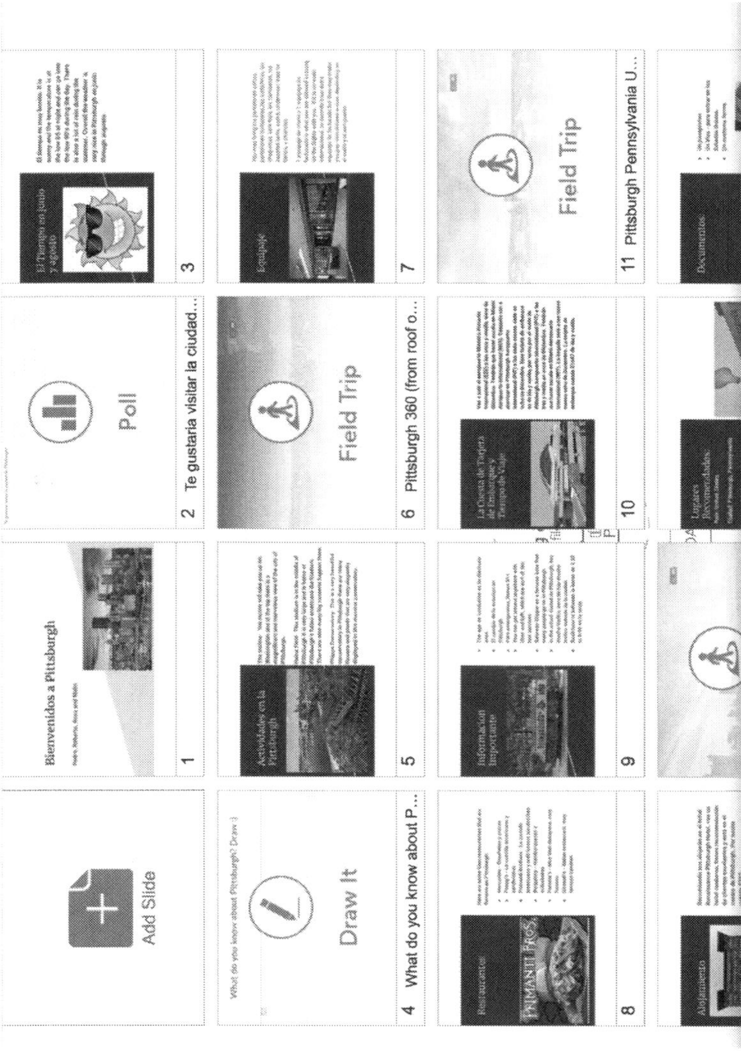

FIGURE 2.7 Nearpod lesson with Virtual Field Trips

functionality so that they can learn about a variety of topics but listen to and read it in the target language

7. Synth (www.gosynth.com) is a tool that we have used for a few years because it provides an easy option for recording a podcast and building communication skills. It can be a great tool for speaking assessments and extending the time and space of classroom discussions. We use Synth with our project-based learning and students were able to ask questions, respond to discussion threads and communicate with students from Argentina and Spain.

Synth includes options to record audio or video. It is a great way to encourage students to share their ideas and build some in speaking. Being able to give students timely and authentic feedback is critical for learning. It is also important that our students be able to provide peer feedback and develop their skills of communicating and collaborating with their classmates. These tools can be helpful to give students the opportunity to build confidence in learning and be able to share through voice or video or combination.

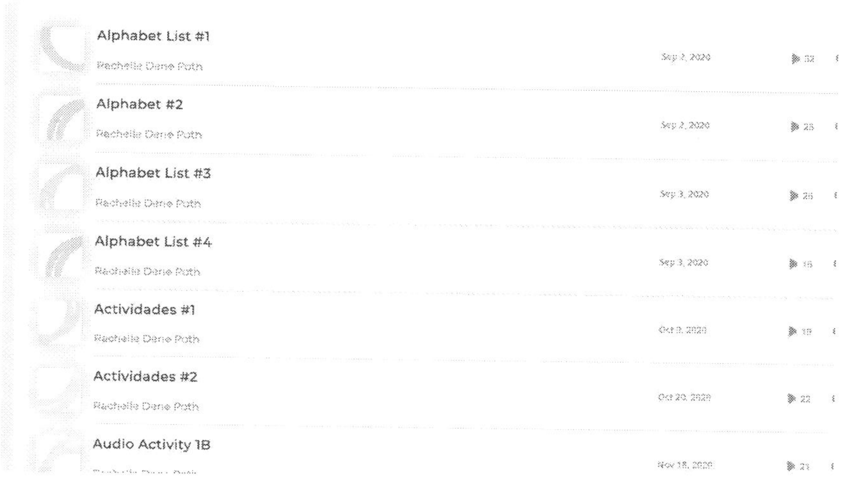

Alphabet List #1

Alphabet #2

Alphabet List #3

Alphabet List #4

Actividades #1

Actividades #2

Audio Activity 1B

FIGURE 2.8 Using Synth to record listening comprehension activities

At the start of the 2020–21 school year, I used some of these tools in different ways because I was struggling to find ways to assess students and be able to provide the right support while we were not in the same physical space. When we were fully remote, I relied more on these digital tools to be able to better provide for my students in a way that was comfortable for them and helped to build their confidence in the language. A few examples were using Flipgrid to do a quick speaking assessment and using Synth to pre-record listening comprehension activities for my students or to provide some practice with the alphabet and pronunciation for them to review. Launching a quick Nearpod lesson made it easy to have students do a quick entrance or exit slip – for example, conjugate verbs or respond to the different prompts that I would give – and enable me to see all of their answers in real-time and be able to adjust my lesson as needed.

Some of these digital tools help students to build confidence in learning and share what they are learning through voice or video or a combination of both. While this is how my students and I have used these tools in our classroom, there are many other tools like them and more ways these tools can be utilized. Think about some of the tasks that might be taking up a lot of your time or consider some issues or challenges you might be having. Ask students for their ideas and see what you learn from them as well.

It has not been easy to transition over the past school year, however we have many tools available to us and we have the opportunity to take some risks and bring in new ideas and possibilities for our students. My recommendation? Start with one thing. Give it a try, ask students for feedback and then make adjustments as needed. New year, new day, and new opportunities for learning!

Ide Koulbanis

One shift was the update to Quizlet Live (www.quizlet.com) that allowed students to play individually and not just on teams. That made it much easier for when we are both in a hybrid model and also in full distance learning mode.

Quizlet Live is another option that gives students more personalized practice as they play the game individually and can review their progress. It also helps us to differentiate instruction for students as they can review the cards after playing the game and we can use it to work with them one-on-one. When in the physical classroom, students enjoy playing on teams and calling out across the room to their teammates as they play to work together on each question. What I have liked about Quizlet Live for so long is that you don't need to project the questions on the screen for all students, so it makes a great choice for anywhere learning. One time we even played a few games on a bus as we traveled to a technology showcase, where students were presenting the Spanish projects they had done and sharing the digital tools they were using. It was a fun activity for students to review and an opportunity to build their collaborative skills and teamwork in the process. It works well for hybrid or virtual environments too!

> **Karina del Castillo**
>
> Working in a virtual environment requires flexibility in our role as educators. I always try to offer different options for those students with little access to electronic facilities. For example, if I need to send a material to print, I will always give the option of allowing the students to make their own version. Or if the task is to make a virtual book using Book Creator, (www.bookcreator.com) I always give students the option to make their book with paper and pencils.
>
> Being flexible allows students to not feel overwhelmed and to have a better performance.

It's Not All About the Technology!

Beyond digital tools, we have so many different methods and strategies that we can try in our classroom. It's important to keep in mind that schools' shifts between hybrid and fully remote learning may continue to be possibilities that we will need to plan for in the future or may be options that we want to provide for our students. We have possibilities that don't require technology at all and simply require some changes to our classroom layout or infusing some creativity and more hands-on learning using traditional materials like paper and pens to help students attach more meaning to what they are learning.

A few years ago, when I noticed student engagement was really low, I struggled to think about what changes I could make in my classroom. I first considered different apps and activities that I could bring in, but nothing seemed to be working. Finally one morning I had a look around my classroom and decided I really didn't like the way that it was set up. So I made some quick changes in the layout of my classroom. I wasn't really sure where to begin but gave it a go and something that has really made a big difference in my own classroom was implementing station rotations.

When I got rid of the rows of desks and created separate groups of desks around the room, it opened up more space where students could really interact with one another and work with peers they may not know very well. Students can be shy or hesitant to work with others, especially when they do not know them well. We all have our sense of comfort and when we can connect with someone that we know, it makes it easier to adapt to a new or uncomfortable situation. By creating these stations randomly, students can develop their interpersonal skills and become more comfortable in their learning environment. It also helped me to be better able to understand their progress in class, to help them to develop their confidence and speaking in front of classmates and engage in conversations with me as well. It also promoted the development of cooperative skills, which lends itself to a welcoming and supportive classroom space.

Grouping students can be an issue, deciding whether to allow students to choose their own groups or not. The best advice is to base it on the students you are working with and maybe start by creating random groups. As a student, I always found working in groups to be somewhat uncomfortable, whether or not I had to pick a partner or was assigned to a specific group. It was always awkward being the only one who doesn't find somebody to work with. Assigning random groups can help to alleviate some of these uncomfortable feelings, even though in life and for the future, students may face some of the same challenges and uncomfortable moments of not having a choice in collaborative work or not being chosen to participate. But we can help to prepare them by planning these activities and working right along with them. Creating more opportunities for students to get to know their peers and to develop more social awareness and understand different perspectives will greatly benefit them as they built their language skills in our classrooms.

Getting Started With Stations

It can be easy to set stations up, depending on your classroom design. With station rotations, try to create groups of desks or "stations" in your classroom, with each station having a designated activity for students to complete before moving to the next station. Figuring out the amount of time for each station can be tricky at first but remember to stay flexible and see how it goes with each group. These are things that we learn as we go, and the great thing about using stations is that we can always come up with different activities for students to work on and it gives us a better chance to work individually with students as well as small groups or the class as a whole.

Get started by explaining how the movement and activities through the rotations will work, provide some guidelines and then just take a chance and see how it goes. Prepare a variety of learning activities to be used at each station. One thing I like to do is include a mix of activities which are hands-on and encourage students to come up with their own ideas. We should offer a mix of hands-on/manipulatives as well as digital tools so that students have the opportunity to learn based on what meets their individual learning styles. It's also important that we use different activities in the stations as a way to better understand our students and their preferences when it comes to learning and to be better able to provide for them in a more personalized way. Leveraging digital tools helps us to provide feedback and to look at each individual student's progress as well as the class as a whole. In using stations, we can take that data and have more time to interact with students one-on-one and work with small groups. In my own experience, I felt like I was teaching every single student every single day. It was making a big difference not just for myself but for students who were telling me how much more they were enjoying the class because of the different ways they had to learn Spanish.

Making It Work

Think about the types of activities you might do with your class as a whole. Would you have a listening comprehension activity or show a video or use a game? Or would you have students complete a worksheet or activity in the textbook, or provide a short lecture about a grammar topic or introducing vocabulary? We do all of these things in our language classrooms, but we may be doing them with the whole class all at the same time. While I believe that some of these activities are great for use with the class as a whole, I've seen in practice in my own classroom that it has been more effective and has greater benefits for my students when they are working in small groups and moving through different activities, especially when I can interact with each of them more closely.

To set up your room, you want to start by deciding on what materials will be needed. Do you want to use class materials, have students create their own materials, use tech tools, play a game or have students decide their own way to practice at that station? Deciding upon the activities takes some planning, especially when trying this for the first time. Don't let this stop you. Remember we are all learners, and it is always good for students to see that it is okay to take a risk by trying something new, to make mistakes and to keep going. Giving up some control in the classroom is not always easy, but the benefit is that it opens up more opportunities for facilitating learning, providing individualized instruction and building those relationships which are the foundation of education today and for life.

Options for Stations: In-Class or Virtual

As we shift between in-person and virtual instruction, it's good to have options available between the tools that we use or the method that we are using in our classroom to provide those personalized learning opportunities for students. When in the classroom, we can have activities at our stations including hands-on manipulatives or worksheets, our direct instruction, and then a variety of interactive options for students to work at their own pace. In my class, I would typically have stations with activities that included making or reviewing flashcards, completing a handout or activity in the book, using an interactive video using something like Edpuzzle, playing review games like Kahoot! (www.kahoot.com) or Quizizz (www.quizizz.com) and sometimes a station for direct instruction, where I would review the material and the activities with the students. Sometimes I would have two stations that might have a Quizizz game with one focused on verb practice and the other focused on vocabulary because I could see each student's progress and also look at the class progress as a whole. Other times I might provide materials like paper, pens, notecards, dry erase boards, dice for the students to come up with their own way to practice. The perfect blend is to mix the traditional materials with the digital, especially when in the physical classroom space.

Now with so many schools working with hybrid learning environments or potentially having to transition, because we spend so much time looking at our screens, it's important to provide choices that help students to break away from the devices and practice the content in meaningful ways. My suggestions are to create a space to post activities for all students using something like Padlet (www.padlet.com), a collaborative digital bulletin board type tool. To facilitate virtual stations, if available, use breakout rooms in Microsoft Teams or Zoom to promote collaborative learning and development of SEL skills. We can have students use paper to write or draw based on a listening comprehension activity as a possibility, and then add in other activities like showing a video, playing a game or creating an interactive lesson. We can also post activities and timers on one of the collaborative board spaces available.

The benefit of stations regardless of where we are learning is that students have the chance to work through a variety of activities that match their learning styles and preferences and that also give us valuable data that we can use as we plan the next lesson. The best part is that it gives students more independence in learning and helps them to move from simply consuming the content to more actively engaging in the learning and building

FIGURE 2.9 Students working in stations

their skills in the target language while also building essential social emotional learning skills in the process. I knew it made a difference when, at the end of the school year, one of my students said, "I feel like I am part of a learning family and I'm really looking forward to next year." If you want to learn more about station rotations and implementing blended learning, I recommend the book *Blended Learning in Action*. Tucker, C. R., Wycoff, T., & Green, J. T. (2017).

When we break from the conventional practices of lecturing or leading for the entire class period, we can spend more time being the facilitator and interacting with our students. When we step back, we give students an opportunity to build their skills and learn to self-assess and we are more accessible to provide the individualized instruction and feedback they need. And remember, the goal in doing this, besides the focus on more authentic and personalized learning, is to help students build those vital connections in the classroom. It is important for us to have that time to really work one-on-one and within those small groups to learn about our students. You will see with each passing week and over the course of the year, the students start to form their own learning networks and your classroom will become a thriving learning community. You will feel the change in your classroom culture, and your students will be even more engaged in learning because they are comfortable and confident in their learning space.

There are a lot of options for using stations in our physical classroom space, but we do also have ways to bring this about in our virtual space. We can use the different features in tools such as Zoom or Microsoft Teams or Google Meet to have breakout rooms. Each breakout room can be assigned to a different task, and we control the amount of time before shifting to another activity. We can use a digital space such as Google Jamboard, Padlet or Wakelet to post the different activities for students to complete. One versatile tool that I find to be quite helpful during learning stations is Classroom Screen. You can use a lot of its features to create a space to let students know time remaining for activities or even to have it choose random names. It also has a feature to randomly assign students to groups, to post a YouTube video and in some cases embed other links to display for class. If you're looking for a quick way to manage time or add some fun extras into class, I recommend checking out Classroom Screen.

FIGURE 2.10 Classroom Screen tool to use for timers and stations

Student in Spanish 1

"One of my favorite tech tools we use is Quizizz because you can not only go at your own pace, but it also turns competitive and adds an enjoyable time to the class! I find that it helps me to practice the language in a different way because it allows me to break down my thought process when choosing the answer without being rushed."

Some of these virtual station options might take a little bit more time to set up at first, but they can be as valuable as doing the stations in our own classrooms.

Through the use of stations we also provide differentiation because we can account for differences in learning styles, interest of students and social-emotional learning needs. It is more student-centered. and we definitely become more flexible in our instruction and have more opportunities for one-on-one instruction. We can also help students to collaborate and pull from their prior knowledge, as they negotiate meaning in the target language and support their peers during these activities. Deborah Blaz (2016) offers some good examples of what differentiated instruction is and some of the possibilities that we can bring into our classrooms. When we use some of these digital tools, we can better track student progress, which is critical for informing our instruction. While we might not be able to do all of the same hands-on activities like playing games or using flashcards, we can still find valuable options for our students to use that break away from technology too.

Movement and SEL!

Beyond using some of the different digital tools and having students complete some hands-on activities, it's also a great idea to get students up and moving when we can. Also bringing in some activities which promote collaboration and communication tied in with the culture of the language that they are studying, we can make connections to personal interests of students or events that are happening in the world. I love this example shared by Katie Bordner, Spanish teacher from Pittsburgh.

March Music Madness

- Based on the NCAA College Basketball Tournament in March (frequently referred to as March Madness) a few groups of Spanish teachers (and French, though I'm not sure about other languages) create a bracket of popular Spanish songs. There are two Spanish teachers that I know of that create different brackets and encourage other teachers to have their students participate in their competition. Justin Buehler creates a bracket using songs that were released within the past 12 months (*https://spanishplans.org/mmm20/*), and Señor Ashby uses any popular song (*www.senorashby.com/locura-de-marzo-2020.html*) that has been nominated by enough teachers into the bracket. Both of these brackets have private Facebook groups where teachers are incredibly generous in sharing materials they've made related to the songs and supportive in talking through the variety of questions that arise when planning lessons.
- The songs are determined beforehand and as a class we preview each song, and each student fills out the bracket making predictions on who is going to win the competition. During March we listen to two songs and vote (online or raising hands) to see which song we liked more. As a school, all the Spanish teachers participate, so we have a "school competition" and compare it to the open global competition. As teachers, we find it builds positive culture in our program and students become invested in popular artists that are in the bracket year after year.
- There are many ways to go deeper than just listening to songs, and it depends on how much time you can spend on the songs. You can discuss the artist, you can "movie talk" the music video, you can complete cloze activities. For the Final Four songs, one year I found Zumba videos for each. One thing I prioritize is speaking in the target language about why we liked/didn't like certain songs and providing them scaffolded language to *explain* their preferences.
- As the competition continues, songs are eliminated and eventually the most popular song wins. Some songs students will love and add to their own playlists, some they hate and it will cause dramatic, highly engaged debates in class. Either way, the community building and increased student voice is a win!

Some Final Ideas to Try!

A few of my most recent favorite additions into my class include some basics like games similar to "Win Lose or Draw" or good old bingo games. Whether we are in our classroom and can use paper or dry erase boards – and when it comes to bingo, printable bingo sheets – or in an online format, having students fill in the words is great practice. I always loved playing bingo as a

Laura Steinbrink, Educator in Missouri

Target Language Spoons!

Supplies needed:

Target Language Vocabulary
Plastic Spoons
Masking Tape
Sharpie
Hand Sanitizer (Pandemic Modification)

Choose a vocabulary word to write on a piece of masking tape and tape it to the spoon. Repeat until you have each vocabulary word on a spoon and a set of spoons for every ten students. At class time, put the spoons in the center of a table for each group. Groups can be smaller than ten students, but it is best not to go over ten. Have the spoons face down so that the vocabulary word can't be seen.

(Pandemic modification: Make sure students use hand sanitizer before beginning.) When you have the class settled and ready, shout out the English version of one of the vocabulary words or shout out the word in the target language, depending on which language you wrote on the tape for the spoons. The student to grab the correct corresponding spoon wins that round.

Repeat until you have gone through all of the vocabulary. Keep score to see which student wins the most rounds for the activity, or have a podium for the top three, real or symbolic. No reward needed other than recognition and cheers, though actual podiums would be cool, like at the Olympics.

Another twist on this is to use it when practicing verb conjugation. Write each verb form on tape and place that on a spoon. It's fun if you use different types of verbs at a time. If teaching Spanish, you would label a spoon for all forms of -ar, -er, and -ir verbs, present tense. When you have the class ready to play in their groups, you shout out a subject. It is so much fun to watch students grab for the correct conjugation on the spoons. Enjoy!

Blog post: *Low Tech High Impact Learning: Spoons As Formative Assessment (https://rockntheboat.com/2020/03/01/low-tech-high-impact-learning-spoons-as-formative-assessment/)*

kid and even now as an adult, there's just something fun about the whole process of it. In my language classes, I would often make a blank bingo sheet and have students fill out words from the vocab and then I would call the words, using a sentence or a clue or using the word in the opposite language. It was a different way to have students engage and have some fun in the classroom. Now with not everybody in the classroom, having digital options that still provide the traditional paper format is great. Bingo Baker has been awesome. However, as with all things, there are a lot of options out there. Two favorites that my students really enjoy using this year are Bingo Baker (www.bingobaker.com) and Skribbl.io.(www.skribbl.io)

Bingo Baker enables you to add your target vocabulary to the card and share a link with students that will generate their own card on their device, or you have the option to print a card. It's really easy to keep track of the words because the teacher or "bingo caller" is provided with the "caller's card" to work through all of the words on the list. Fun for students in the class and students at home. This works whether everybody's together or in hybrid or fully virtual learning. You might wonder, "How do I know if students truly have a bingo?" That's when we make sure they know how to share their screen, building skills in the content and building skills in technology too.

With Skribbl.io, you can add your own vocabulary words in the target language and then give a join code for students to become part of the game. Each person gets a chance to draw while the others have to guess what the object is by writing the word in the target language. Players cannot see the word that was guessed, if another player was correct. Either way, these two games offer a lot of possibilities for building language skills, especially because they're giving students the chance to interact with the content in different ways, whether by drawing and associating the words with the meaning or from the process of thinking about the word being called in bingo and then searching for it and marking it on their card. What I did with the bingo game is I made up sentences or clues in the target language and had students search for the word or phrase that I was referring to. It took a little bit of quick thinking on my part, but it was a lot of fun to build their vocabulary or verb skills but also to have them focus on their listening skills in class.

It really doesn't take a lot of technology or spending a lot of time to find new ideas. Sometimes we can take a game that we've already played in the past or ask students to help us make one up, whatever it is that helps them to create and interact with the content in different ways.

In this chapter hopefully you gathered a lot of new ideas, whether it's a new tool or strategy, or perhaps a tool that you were already using but you learned a new way to use it in the classroom. We can come up with a lot of innovative ways to help students build their language skills, and we can also learn a lot from students about what helps them to learn best. Pick a few of these and try them in your classroom. Ask for student feedback often. Involving them in the process shows them that we value their input and helps us to make sure that we are providing the right resources and practice to support development of skills in the target language.

3

Fostering Strong Communication Skills in Our Students

Chapter Summary:

In this chapter you will learn strategies and tools for fostering better communication skills in our students. Beyond the development of language skills in our classroom, students need to learn how to communicate and collaborate with one another in various settings, contexts and using different media formats. Through the use of different digital tools and teaching strategies, we can help students to build confidence and peer collaborations in the classroom and connect our classroom on a global scale. Through the use of digital tools which promote communication and collaboration, such as blogging, video creation and podcasting, we can enhance student learning by creating more meaningful connections and providing different formats for students to convey their thoughts. The ideas shared will be applicable to in-person and remote learning and can be put into practice quickly. Learn how to make slight shifts in teaching strategies to help students develop these essential skills.

What to expect in this chapter:

- Ideas for promoting communication and collaboration between students

DOI: 10.4324/9781003137665-4

- Tools that are beneficial for in-person, hybrid or fully virtual learning
- Options to move students from consumers to creators with the language

With so much of our school experience relying on technology and setting up virtual learning spaces for students, we have to be intentional about finding ways to promote communication and collaboration between students and ourselves. Especially as we may be working through changing learning environments, we need to set up a consistent way for students to communicate their learning with us and with each other. In the absence of in person interactions, we must leverage the different strategies and tools available to us to help create our presence in and out of the classroom space. There are different ways that teachers as well as students can develop and maintain a social presence in an online learning environment, and it is important that we decide on what that might look like for the students in our classroom. How can we leverage different digital tools and virtual spaces to enhance the communication that is happening?

In my own experience as an online learner when getting my master's degree, it took time to adapt to that experience of not being in the same physical space as the teacher or other students. Deciding how to communicate and collaborate with classmates took time. I will share examples from my experiences as a student and some which I have implemented in my classroom. A few examples include sending welcome emails, posting a welcome message on the class website, or recording a video introduction. Each of these are good ways to set up an initial connection with students and families. At the start of the year or throughout the year, doing ice-breaker activities can enhance communication and facilitate the building of relationships between students and teachers. Creating discussion boards with guided questions encourages more interactions, and posting comments and responses to one another in discussion threads are also beneficial ways to infuse the learning environment with interactive communication and collaboration.

Even in the absence of being in the same physical space, we can communicate our personality and show excitement, passion and investment in student learning through online mediums. Classes which are asynchronous can be more difficult because of the time lapse that occurs in between synchronous interactions, so we need to be intentional about designing opportunities for communication and collaboration to occur. We need different tools to help express our ideas, convey what we are learning, exchange questions and foster relationships to interact in online spaces. To promote communication, especially in asynchronous environments, choosing a few tools that offer multiple ways to communicate in the target language will engage students more in active and meaningful learning.

In order to help students develop their language skills, we need tools in our toolkit that encourage and support students with reading, writing, listening and speaking in the target language. By implementing a few multipurpose tools, we have the opportunity to extend those discussions beyond the class, and we should take those opportunities to amplify the learning possibilities for all students. These collaborations can go beyond class time and space by implementing some of the different tools to encourage students to engage in conversations not only with their peers but with global peers around the world. It is important that we help students to build their social presence, especially whenever we are not in our classroom space. We need to help them to learn how to navigate in the virtual space to not only connect with classmates and the content that they're learning but to prepare them for their future.

When I was working my master's degree, it was the first time that I took online classes. It felt different because of the lack of personal interactions with classmates and not being able to have conversations and interact with one another in a real classroom. It was difficult to make connections initially until the professor added a live class session and we could actually see each other. What a difference that made. As I've been teaching virtually and in hybrid for the past year and anticipate that we will continue to provide this type of instruction, I've often recalled how different that first online course experience was for me. Prior to the live class session, I didn't know anything about classmates or the instructor beyond their names and information shared on the discussion board or shared through email. It was difficult to understand somebody's tone from only written communication. After that first live interaction, it helped to make communication between the instructor and myself and the other students feel more natural. Because of my experience with many online courses, I've tried to find unique and innovative ways to help my students feel more connected to one another and better able to communicate in an online learning experience.

Questions to consider:

1. How do you communicate in the online space with educators and students?
2. What do you notice about these communications? Are there opportunities to exchange ideas in multiple formats? Are there spaces to interact with others and build relationships?
3. How can we encourage students to communicate more in ways that meet their comfort and build their confidence in learning?

With remote learning and the uncertainty of how school might look as we face each school year, we need to put in place ways to continue building the relationships that we create during the school year. Being able to see each other and make those connections is important. During the 2020–21 school year, in my own classroom and in many classrooms around the world, as educators engaged in fully remote or hybrid learning, they shared the challenges of teaching in these spaces. Most common shared experiences were of students who would turn off their cameras, which made it feel awkward at times. Without the opportunity to see one another, it feels like we are not talking to anybody and there are no visual cues to help us understand if students comprehend the content and our conversations do not feel as authentic and natural. However, it is important to respect the privacy of students who decide to keep their cameras off. In my classes, as long as students were responsive, I was mostly okay with that. But I enjoy being able to see one another as we talk, so I started doing "Friday faces."

Students were quick to know what I meant, and they humored me. I wanted them to turn on their cameras so I could see them and they could see one other. Even though it was for only a minute or two, it made a difference for everyone to see and hear each other. Even a quick visual interaction can make a difference and it always brought a smile to my face. Having a space to connect, to collaborate and communicate while also building confidence in the language is important.

Facilitating Online Discussions and Chats

While in virtual or hybrid, we have to select some additional tools to make these interactions happen. There are a lot of options that work well regardless of grade level and that we can implement quickly into our lessons. Here are some of those that I have used in my classroom and some ideas shared by members of my professional learning network (PLN).

A few years ago, I looked for some options to encourage conversation between students from different classes and also to use for setting up virtual office hours to be available for my students. The options that I will share worked well for that purpose, especially as a language teacher, for supporting students as they build their skills and need support during that process. In particular for hybrid learning, using backchannel discussion tools and other digital tools to foster conversations between all students is beneficial and can easily be added into our toolkit for creating new ways to collaborate.

With the rise of new technologies and digital tools, we don't have the same limits on learning as in the past. We now have the opportunity to provide different learning spaces for our students that provide them with more time to explore, communicate and build the essential skills that will best prepare them for when they leave our schools. We can also provide more student choice by offering multiple ways for students to share learning and build confidence and collaborative skills in the process. So how can we encourage students to communicate and share their learning beyond the traditional classroom space and time?

Here are ten options and some suggested tools that can promote student choice, foster the development of digital citizenship and social-emotional learning skills and extend learning to meet students' interests and needs. By starting with one or two of these options, we can learn from our students and empower them to be creators rather than just consumers in our classrooms. Students can decide which format best fits their needs and interests and use it as a starting point to build skills in more personalized ways. We just need to know enough to get our students started and then give them the opportunity to create, explore and make it their own.

For educators, these additional options enable us to provide the authentic, specific and timely feedback that is critical for student growth. These tools can be used to facilitate global collaboration between classrooms, which promotes cultural awareness and creates a more authentic and meaningful learning experience for students. My classroom has collaborated with schools in Argentina and Spain using similar tools, and it has made a lasting impact on my students and their motivation for language learning.

Sharing Ideas, Collaborating, Brainstorming and More!

Backchannel Discussion Spaces

a. Looking for a different way to assess students and be able to provide feedback faster, I first explored GoSoapBox (www.gosoapbox.com) with my Spanish III students. For a midterm exam, I gave students the option to try GoSoapBox for entering their responses rather than writing on paper. My purpose was that I wanted a better way to be able to see their work and also to more quickly provide feedback. Student feedback was very positive and so I decided to expand on that original use of it. I created "events" and used the space to share responses with other students, to promote peer collaboration and peer feedback. With GoSoapBox you can create a poll, quiz or discussion, and it is free to use and easy to get started with. If you are looking for a quick way to gather some responses without requiring logins or any downloads, I recommend exploring GoSoapBox.

Over the years I have also used some tools for backchannel discussions and for connecting with other classrooms and colleagues globally. Each of these work well for synchronous or asynchronous learning. Some of the additional tools that work well are: Backchannel Chat (www.backchannelchat.com), Padlet (www.padlet.com), Parlay (www.parlayideas.com) and Yo Teach! (www.yoteachapp.com). The benefit of these choices is that as students work on activities to practice the content or work on a project together, providing one accessible space for all students to interact makes a difference. As many of us may use a learning management system (LMS) or perhaps Google Classroom or Microsoft Teams, these options promote more collaborative learning that benefit hybrid and fully virtual learning and also enhance the conversations happening during in-person instruction. Using something like Backchannel Chat or Yo Teach! gives the students a chance to not only ask the questions but potentially to provide responses to questions from their classmates. When we create these spaces, we help students to feel valued in learning and build confidence in creating with the language. It also empowers students to develop their self-advocacy, digital citizenship and SEL skills in the process, all of which are vital for the future.

b. When looking for ideas to help students engage in a discussion, it is helpful if we can make connections with events that are happening in the world. When students can draw from their experiences or perhaps consider current events, for example, it helps them to develop their language skills in more authentic ways. It also builds upon what they have learned in class, whether we come up with the ideas for them or we use a tool such as Parlay, which offers different choices to connect students with real-world issues and expand the types of conversations we are having in our classroom. Teachers can create their own questions or topics for class discussion or select a topic from the available library. Parlay allows students to join in a live roundtable discussion and then continue the conversation asynchronously. We can help students through scaffolding by having them review relevant class materials, submit responses and collaborate with peers to give each other feedback.

   Promoting conversations is important for students to develop not only their speaking skills but listening and interpersonal skills as well. We can use Parlay to extend discussions using a Socratic-style method. Teachers can access data and can provide more personalized and timely feedback to students. With platforms like this that have topics and resources readily available, it helps us to bring in more current and relevant issues to help students develop communication skills, extend vocabulary as well as negotiate meaning through circumlocution.

c. Another way to build communication skills and extend discussions beyond the class period or for balancing with hybrid teaching is to use Backchannel Chat (www.backchannelchat.com). There have been many class periods, especially in the hybrid learning environment, where students may have questions and the class period ends or students simply didn't have the chance to ask a question. As a result, students leave without having the clarification that they need or validation of something that they might not have understood well and were still trying to process. Finding a way to be available while balancing the demands of hybrid instruction can take some time. However, using a tool like Backchannel Chat or other similar tools, enables us to create a space where students can ask and even answer the questions of their classmates and they can do so beyond the limits of the class period.

As with all technologies we bring into our classroom, we need to help students to build responsible digital citizenship skills and to be respectful of interacting together in the online space and leveraging these spaces to build our classroom community. One of the features of Backchannel Chat is that teachers can delete responses if needed and even lock the chat room so that only the teacher is adding content to the discussion or as a way to slow down the pace of the discussion. Another idea is to use a tool like this for students to brainstorm or collaborate on a project and have a space to share their resources or engage in conversations to practice their writing and reading skills in the language. The only requirement is that teachers create a chat room for students to use.

We increase our availability by having access to the chat discussion even after the class period ends, which helps us stay better connected with our students. We do have to set some boundaries when it comes to availability, but for myself, I choose to make

FIGURE 3.1 Tools available in the Spaceboard of Yo Teach!

these tools available to students and I respond as soon as I can. As long as students can access resources or ask questions when they need to and they know that their questions will be answered, then having set times is definitely possible. These options for communicating also give students the chance to step in, lead the discussion and provide support to their classmates. Students build leadership skills and become better and more confident communicators.

d. Saving time and getting started quickly with some of these ideas is key, and that is why I also enjoy using Yo Teach! Similar to Backchannel Chat, teachers can quickly create a chat room and post questions, moderate discussions and have control over who is communicating within the chat room. It gives students the chance to have conversations, focus on their written communication as well as their reading comprehension skills in responding and provides a different media that we can use to help students to build their language skills. There are additional interactive features in Yo Teach! that would be fun for language classes.

Here Are Four Ideas for Yo Teach!

- Submit a drawing, which can be fun for language classes.
- Build vocabulary skills by asking students to draw in response to a sentence, single vocabulary word, or phrase in the target language.
- Create a poll to do a quick assessment on how students feel about their progress or if they have any questions about

material. Using anonymous polls help students to feel more confident in expressing if they need additional help or perhaps have students vote on a topic of discussion for class.

- Start a discussion about a topic that has pros/cons or assign students to take one side of an argument and use the space to share opinions and ask questions.

It is nice to have another free digital option that promotes more collaboration between students and is beneficial for fostering the development of social-emotional learning skills. Yo Teach! also offers some newer features that make it a really great space for collaboration. You can create a room and set a password for students to log in. The options available enable participants to send a message in text, add in a poll, create a collaborative Spaceboard or upload a picture to share. Within the settings, you can set text to be read, mute participants, mark a post as a good question and reverse the order of posts. With the collaborative space, there are lots of possibilities, from demonstrating how to conjugate verbs to having students work together in that same space to do something like a scavenger hunt for brainstorming ideas. There are many possibilities when learning a language!

Collaborative Spaces for Learning

e. Whiteboard Chat. While we are not all in the same physical classroom space, having options where we can collaborate with our students and they can collaborate together has been so beneficial for keeping students connected and

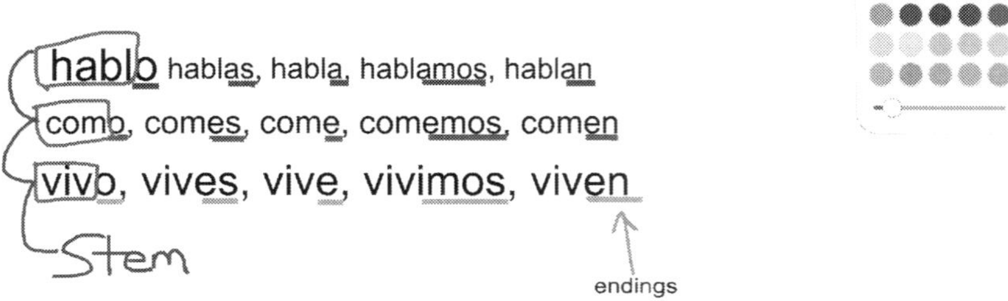

FIGURE 3.2 Different ways to create in Yo Teach!

> being able to provide more active learning experiences. It is even better when we can find tools which are free and easy to get started with. A very robust tool that I recommend all language teachers check out is Whiteboard.chat. I started to use it with my students, and there are so many possibilities for using it in any classroom. You can either create a whiteboard that you share with students or provide individual whiteboards for students to use that you can view as they are working on them.

It only took me a few minutes to explore the many possibilities with it, including having students draw, which is great for having them conjugate verbs. I found it to be quite useful for uploading documents for my students to work on and then giving them time to respond or draw. It helps to simulate what would happen in the physical classroom by creating a space where all students can work and feel part of the class. There are more than 100 options of tools and activities that you can bring into the whiteboard space. You can choose from a variety of drawing and writing tools, backgrounds, emojis and more. To save time, you can upload multiple pages that enable students to annotate the pages or complete activities which you can see in real-time. To provide more personalized learning experiences as students work, there is the video call feature for providing feedback to students.

Two features that are really standouts are the Immersive Reader and "Time Machine." Having the ability to translate for students and to provide additional language learning support, especially when looking at accessibility tools, is pretty phenomenal. There are more than 120 languages available within Whiteboard.chat. The Time Machine feature enables teachers to look at the student's progress over a specific time or to see the work as they are doing it, and then be able to provide better feedback and support for them.

It comes down to personal preference and considering what you are looking for in some of these different digital tools. If you want something simpler with fewer choices, then perhaps starting with Yo Teach! might be the best option. If you are looking to provide a lot of different types of content, with fun additions like having dice roll on the screen, creating different shapes or drawings and embedding YouTube videos right within the space, then I would choose Whiteboard.chat. It is a great choice for hybrid learning, especially so that students can work together on the same space and for teachers to be able to see the work and activities in real time.

Here are a few other ideas for some collaborative spaces that offer some similar possibilities as those mentioned but, depending on your school's resources or network, some of these options may not necessarily be made available to you.

f. Draw.Chat (www.draw.chat) is an online whiteboard that provides a free space to have a collaborative drawing that can be used during classes or even for meetings. You can draw, chat or even communicate with others through audio and video conferencing. Educators will also appreciate that you can upload a PDF and have students annotate on it. If you have some practice worksheets or other handouts that are not easily shared with students due to hybrid or virtual learning, you can upload them into Draw.Chat and provide activities for students to make it more interactive and also promote accessibility to resources. You can also upload images or a GIF to the space, which are great for having students write creatively or for a quick discussion prompt. Why not choose an image that sparks some curiosity or use it as a hook for the class lesson? Encourage students to do a free write on it or to even use some other tools for speaking or podcasting to explain what they think about the prompt.

The spaces or "projects" that you create in Draw.Chat are stored for at least one month. It is also helpful that Draw.Chat can be used on the phone without any time at all to get started, which makes it a popular choice for educators who are looking to implement a tool without losing a lot of instructional time or worrying about accessibility on different devices for students. Tools which are accessible on multiple devices are always a plus for

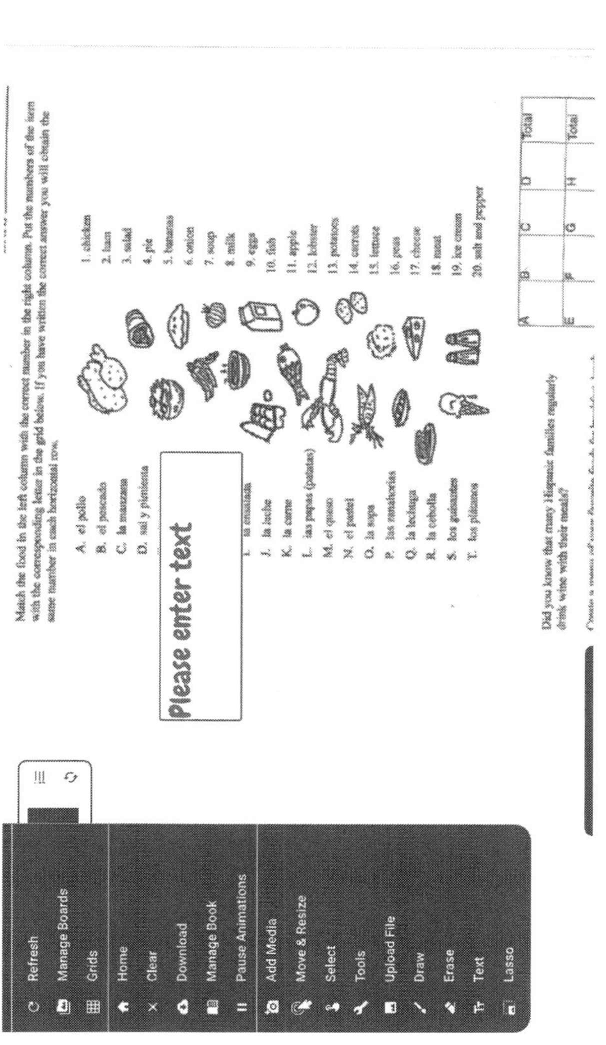

FIGURE 3.3 Toolbars and options in Whiteboard.chat

classrooms. I recommend checking out all of its features first and making sure it meets security requirements for your students. It is also a good option to use as a way to collaborate with other language educators to share ideas, especially globally and when we cannot be in the same space as our colleagues or meeting in person at local events and conferences.

g. Google Jamboard has become another widely popular choice among educators around the world who have been sharing all of the different ways that it can be used in the classroom. Jamboard is a free, cloud-based interactive whiteboard system that teachers can use to design more collaborative and visually engaging learning experiences. It took only a few minutes to set up a Jamboard for each of my Spanish classes to try, and my students figured out exactly what to do without needing much direction from me.

Here Are Some Ideas That Will Be Fun Using Jamboard

If you are using Google Meet or Microsoft Teams or a similar meeting platform, create breakout rooms and have students complete a collaborative task on the Jamboard. By having breakout rooms, in addition to being able to collaborate on the whiteboard space, students can also have conversations, and hearing each other's voices definitely makes a difference for learning. My Spanish II students shared their midterm projects in their small breakout rooms and then posted what they learned on the Jamboard. I chose to have students do presentations this way since we were working in a hybrid model, and I wanted all students to be able to participate but also to be able to have conversations and engage more meaningfully with their classmates. I also believe that by using small groups like this, it helps students to build comfort and confidence in speaking in front of their classmates and will help them to become even more comfortable speaking in front of peers or to the class as a whole.

How did it go? My students enjoyed working in small groups and posting additional notes and images on the Jamboard. I took time to check in on each breakout room and give some guidance about posting on the Jamboard, but students did not need much direction from me. They were naturally taking the lead, assigning tasks and speaking in Spanish! I also used it with Spanish III to provide an image as a prompt and asked each group to describe the scene using their current chapter vocabulary and verbs.

Jamboard doesn't require much planning. I decided to do a quick scavenger hunt with my Spanish I students who were studying foods vocabulary. A few minutes before class started, I decided to create a quick Jamboard and instructed my students to explore their kitchen and find any products or packages of foods that had Spanish written on them. They were to post an image onto the Jamboard and write a short sentence about their preferences or likes, using *gustar* and *preferir*, new verbs we were working with. We then had a discussion about the items added to the Jamboard, and it became a more real-world experience to see and apply language skills. It was a more active learning experience and added more authenticity to what they were learning because they could see the posts of classmates and be able to experience more real world learning. Google Jamboard is free to use, easy to get started with, and is a great option for whether you are in person, hybrid or fully virtual learning.

Here Are Ten Quick Ideas to Try Using Any of the Collaborative Spaces Shared Above

1. Create a scavenger hunt and have each group post on one space within the same Jamboard or whiteboard, and then you can use it to add to the discussion, asking students to describe what they see using the target language.
2. Use it as a space to have students respond to prompts and engage in a conversation with classmates.
3. Post an image and encourage students to write a narration or caption.

FIGURE 3.4 Students posting on Jamboard based on image prompts

4. Ask students to post a question or curiosity on the board and encourage other students to respond to one another using text or notes.
5. Design a flipped or blended learning experience by posting activities or even station activities on the board space.
6. Use a Jamboard or chatboard space to provide instructions and activities for students to follow.
7. Create sections on the board and ask students to post their name on a note near where their preferences are and explain. List foods, activities, travel locations and preferences, school information and more!
8. Use it as a space to have students post verbs or vocabulary in the target language. A fun way to practice verbs, create sentences and then use it for conversations in class.
9. Pick a topic and ask students to place related words on the board. This can be a good way to keep reviewing a lot of the different vocabulary and verbs throughout the year.
10. PBL brainstorm space: Have students list topics they would like to explore, then use it to group students and provide the space for students to share resources and add ideas!

Collaboration Time

Whether in person or through digital instruction, it's important to create spaces for students to engage in conversations, provide peer feedback or work together on a group project, for example. We need to hear each other's voices to build our speaking and listening skills and be able to see each other so we can have more personal interactions and build relationships. Building interpersonal skills is important. When in the classroom, we can use different teaching strategies or classroom design, like stations, that give students a chance to work together and enables us to have more opportunities to interact with each student and each

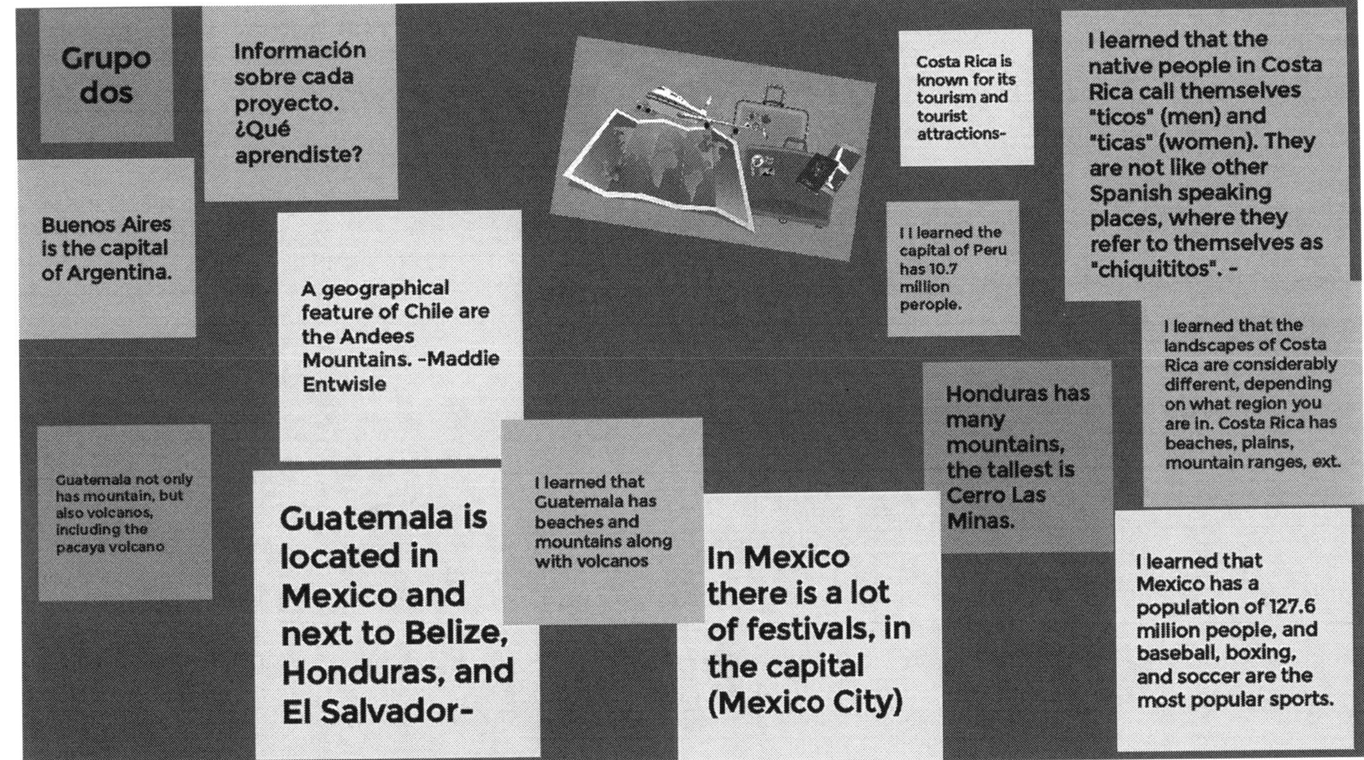

FIGURE 3.5 Students worked in breakout rooms on Microsoft Teams to present projects, then shared on Google Jamboard

group. In the digital environment, we can select from many of the digital tools for providing collaborative spaces for our students.

There are many possibilities for collaboration in virtual spaces, starting with some of the video tools available to us. We can use our meeting platforms to arrange time to be available online for students to answer their questions or to provide feedback to them, which is a great way to stay connected. The best part of each day is always the interactions we have with students, whether this happens in our classroom space and we greet students as they enter, we provide opportunities for them to interact with one another in class or we create this experience in the digital space. These collaborative experiences are important for student growth in many areas. It is important that we find a way to be available when students need us and a way for them to work together.

Depending on the resources available within our schools, we may be using Google Meet, Microsoft Teams or Zoom. There are other options available to us, including using some video response tools, a few of the whiteboard collaborative spaces or we can set up meeting spaces through other tools such as Skype. Leveraging the many possibilities available to us through these technologies is key.

So why is this important? When we shift to virtual learning, and this is something that I experienced in my own work as a student, we lose out on social interactions. If we are interacting solely by exchanging our ideas through writing in an online space, without any opportunity for audio or video interactions, it makes it more difficult to truly connect. This lack of social presence has been a concern in regard to online learning for a long time, and as a language educator, it is so important to create these spaces for our students. There are many ways that educators can promote the development of social presence and help students to develop their communicative and interpersonal skills by leveraging some of the digital tools available.

As language educators, we also need to provide comprehensible input. Stephen Krashen's theory of comprehensible input (CI) is an influential theory of second language acquisition. CI is a language that students can understand. We use a variety of language input including listening to audio recordings, conversations and podcasts, for example, or reading blogs, books other written communication. Language acquisition happens better not just when we read or listen to something that is easy for us to understand, it is best and more effective when the input is slightly more advanced than the learner's own level. It helps that we have a lot of possibilities for different types of media to choose from to bring into our classrooms. As language educators, since we are focusing on the four skills of listening, reading, writing and speaking, we need to provide a variety of opportunities for students to choose something that meets their comfort level and interest while helping them to build confidence in learning.

Fostering Speaking and Listening Skills

To provide comprehensible input in forms that build these skills in the target language, here are some additional options for formats and tools:

> The use of podcasting has so many benefits and, in particular for language learners, provides opportunities to build speaking and listening skills. However, we can also use it to promote writing skills by having students respond to what they are hearing or perhaps use it as a way to have students take a dictation to the conversation. Personally, I had always thought about having students do their own podcast, but I held off because I wanted to create my own first so that I was better prepared to help them. My problem was that I wasn't sure what I would talk about. Finally one day, I got started by using Synth and simply recording some of my thoughts as a short podcast and pressing publish, to share it with others. I have been recording my own podcast for a few years. The benefits are that even though it's just me talking, I find that it is great for sharing my ideas, reflecting on my work, and these could also be good experiences for our students.

Years ago, I had a Google Voice number for students to use for recording speaking assessments. It worked very well because I could listen to all of their responses more easily. Then I found Synth and shifted to using it for speaking assessments. Using this method gave them more comfort in knowing that they could record in their own home and redo it if needed. It provided one space for all of their conversations. Podcasting also became a way for students to have conversations with native Spanish speakers. By sharing our podcast link, students from Argentina and Spain could respond by adding a thread to the conversation. Seeing the other students building their English-speaking skills helped my students to feel much more comfortable when speaking in Spanish. My students also appreciated the opportunity to listen to the podcasts of other students, which improved their listening comprehension skills and vocabulary usage.

Where to Begin

h. Podcasting: Start a podcast to provide class updates, share ideas, or just talk using free tools like Synth (www.gosynth.com) or Anchor (www.anchor.fm). Educators can record messages to help students to build their listening skills or create a discussion topic and have students respond to a thread using audio or video (depending on the platform) as they choose. Being able to see and hear directly from classmates and colleagues, especially in the absence of being in the same physical space during hybrid or virtual learning, can make a big difference in the learning experience and helps us to feel more connected. I have also used *Anchor* (https://anchor.fm/rdene915) to share ideas on a variety of topics, and it is very easy to get started with. If each student creates their own podcast where they talk about different topics, perhaps some of which you provide to them or ones that they come up with on their own, it's another authentic way to build speaking skills in a comfortable space. We can use the space to provide feedback directly to them.

Even though it is asynchronous, it's a good way to have a conversation and opens up more possibilities for being able to communicate with each of our students, especially when the limits of the class period and space do not allow us to do so as often as we would like.

i. Videos for learning: A big concern is how to provide ongoing instruction and support for our students. We can leverage some of the different tools available for creating short videos that we can share and make them available for students and share with other language educators around the world. Leveraging some of these screen recording tools helps us to better communicate ideas for students and offers a resource that our students can refer to as they build their skills. There are many free tools out there and some which have free accounts with limits. Some that I have used are Screencastify (www.screencastify.com), Screencast-o-matic (www.screencast-o-matic.com) and Loom (www.loom.com). Flipgrid also can be used to record a lesson up to a ten-minute limit.

j. Student-created lessons: Other options for creating instructional videos are tools like Educreations (www.educreations.com) or ShowMe (www.showme.com), where you can use an interactive whiteboard or add images to your lesson. For a quick video recording, a simple Google search can help you to find a webcam recorder which can be used to record and then download an mp4 of your video to share on other platforms. Depending on the age of our students, they can also create their own videos to talk about what they are learning. It gives them another way to be creative with the language while building some vital technology skills in the process. I've had students teach a lesson about verbs or vocabulary using Educreations. This gives more meaning to what students are creating, and it provides us with more resources for our classroom and to share with other students.

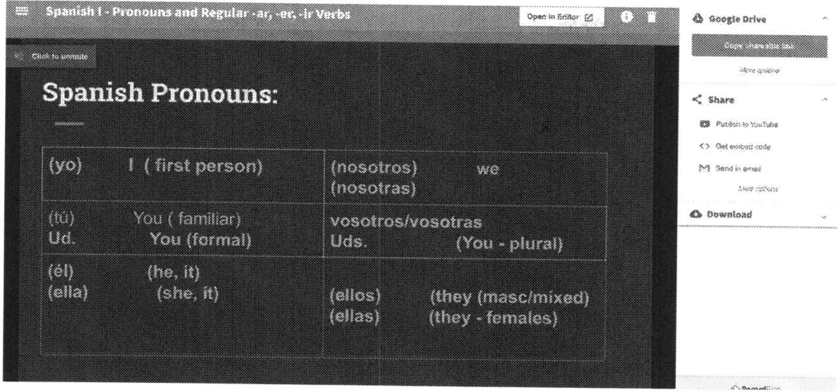

FIGURE 3.6 Lesson recorded in Screencastify and options for sharing

Connecting through Multimedia: The amount of technology available to us as educators continues to grow each day. With new technology comes many opportunities that years ago, would have taken a lot of time to get started with or would have required multiple components. In 2010, my school received rechargeable cameras that students could use to quickly create and edit some videos. It was perfect because at that time, students did not all have cellphones with the capabilities that we have today. I couldn't wait to use them and give students the opportunity to work in small groups and create their own TV program or movie trailer. The activity came at the perfect time of the year, at the end of the spring when students were feeling a little less motivated and student engagement was down. The group video activity presented a tremendous opportunity for more active learning that was student-driven. It also promoted the development of SEL skills as they worked together to design their group video.

When students submitted their work, it was fun to see what each group had created. Their video creations gave me better insight into my students and their interests and definitely a new appreciation for their creativity. It led me to realize that I needed to provide more multimedia options for learning for my students and, in particular, ones that they were responsible for creating. For more interactive learning options that can include a variety of media and promote collaboration, tools mentioned earlier like Buncee, Flipgrid and Padlet are great for creating activities, announcements, lessons and more by leveraging the many options available within each of them.

> **Luis Oliveira, Director of Unified Arts/ELL Teacher, Middletown High School, Rhode Island**
>
> Using multiple programs or apps (app smashing) is a way of having students demonstrate more than one of the language domains. For example, using Buncee or PowerPoint to create their #OneWord at the start of a new year and then using Flipgrid to orally discuss their word choice while using the image they created. My students also did this when discussing their wishes for the world and what they were thankful for.

Kristen and Luis share wonderful ideas for helping students to build their speaking skills and also collaborating with peers. It is always good to have options like these that offer many possibilities for language learners. Another tool that is quite versatile that we use often is Wakelet. Wakelet (www.wakelet.com) is a content curation tool and so much more. Initially I used it as a "space" where I would curate blogs, videos and other resources, which made it easier to find everything rather than sorting through a list of links. It has become a powerful tool for student learning. With Wakelet, teachers can design blended learning experiences, use it for station rotation activities, have students create a digital portfolio, create a scavenger hunt (my friend Laura Steinbrink, educator in Missouri, did this) and many other possibilities. You can also record a Flipgrid short video that is embedded right within the Wakelet collection. Educators and students can collaborate in a Wakelet collection and even fully embed a Buncee presentation into the Wakelet! Wakelet launched a feature called "Spaces" which creates even more possibilities for collaboration by enabling educators to collaborate in the same space. We used it as a space to share PBL projects and resources for our class.

> **Kristen Lyon, Spanish Teacher, Middletown High School, Rhode Island**
>
> Language classes are all about communication. My AP students complete a cultural comparison on holiday traditions. They created visuals using Buncee and then recorded the two-minute comparison on Flipgrid. Students were then able to respond to one another on Flipgrid.

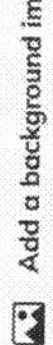

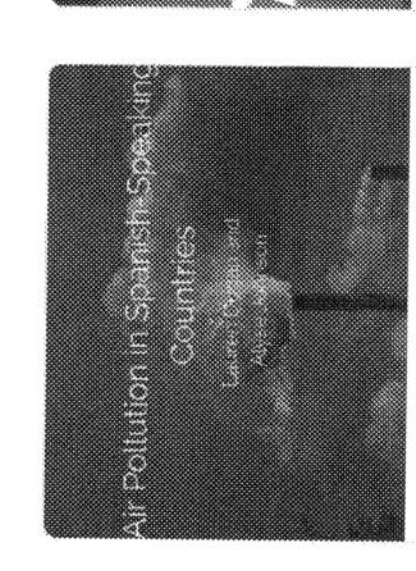
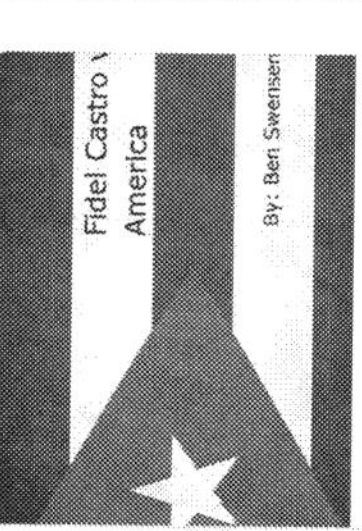

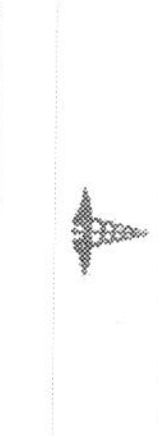

FIGURE 3.7 Sharing PBL projects on Wakelet

Creating Spaces for Collaborating and More!

As mentioned earlier, Whiteboard.chat is a great addition to your tech toolkit. It has Immersive Reader and it's free.

When creating your Whiteboard space, you can set it to have a password for students to join. You can also share through QR code or even duplicate the different whiteboards spaces for use in other classes. There are many choices available in the toolbar on the left for animating the images on the screen and including images, references and videos. Using the different Whiteboard Chat tools, teachers can design a lesson and screen share, which enables us to provide additional support during class and have the class material available beyond the class period. Whatever is added to the Whiteboard space can easily be downloaded and saved for later access for students. This is great especially for whenever we are not in the same class or space. Being able to see the student progress as they work and being able to act on that and give them authentic and timely feedback is critical.

Some activities that you can do with Whiteboard.chat:

- Upload a worksheet or even multiple pages for students to have their own workspace where they can write and you can see their work in real time.
- Have students respond to prompts or brainstorm ideas with classmates, maybe for PBL or a theme to explore together.
- Schedule a quick video call to help students one-on-one.
- Include a YouTube video and activities for students to complete and use the space to create blended or flipped learning experiences.
- Add an image to the whiteboard space and ask students to describe it in the target language.
- Post sentences in the target language and ask students to draw as a way to interpret the meaning.

In the end, we know there are many options available that can be very beneficial for practicing in the target language and helping students to feel more closely connected to each other and the

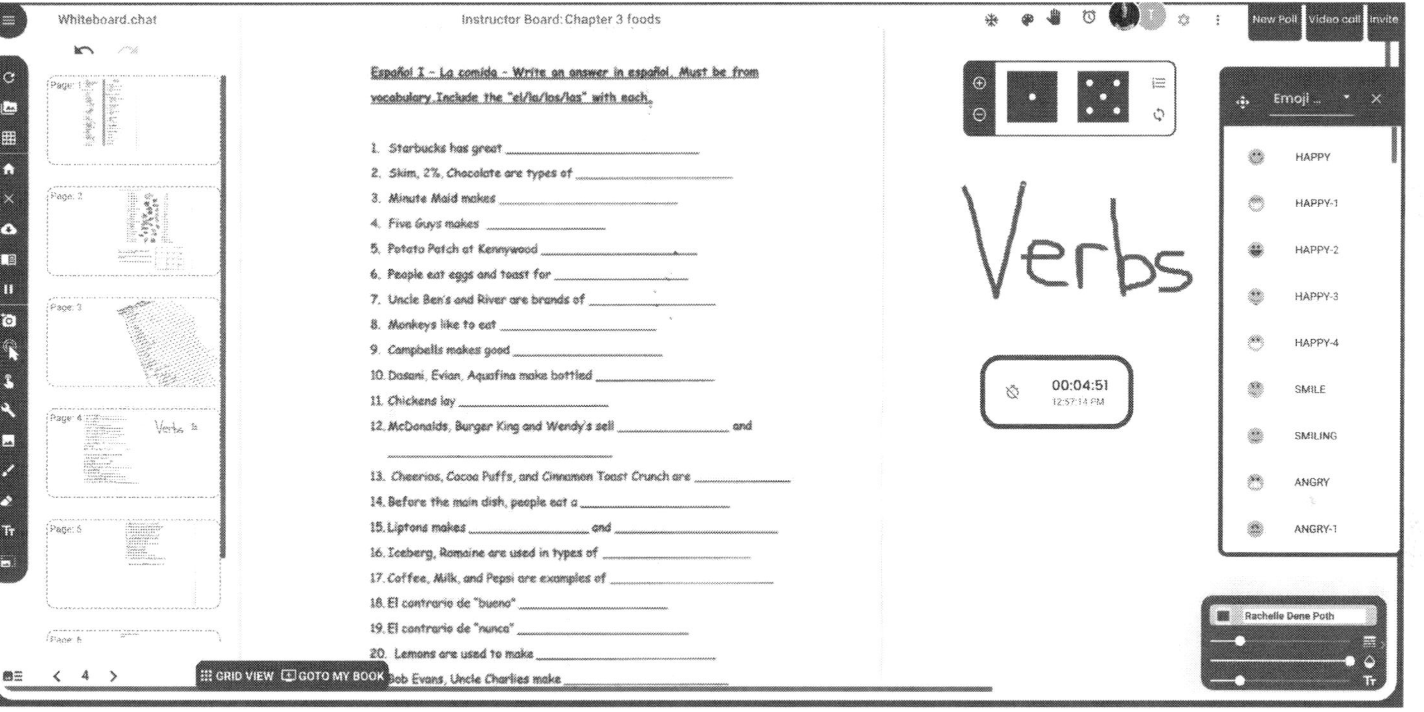

FIGURE 3.8 A look at some of the possibilities available through Whiteboard.chat

learning experience. We simply need to choose one or two to explore and take time to evaluate the benefits, seek feedback from students and then plan our next steps.

Deciding Where to Begin

There are many activities that we can bring into our language classrooms that help students to build their language skills in a variety of ways. The options I describe enable us to take something that might be a traditional activity or game and tweak it so that it fits with the content that we are teaching. But perhaps even more than that, these tools give students more of an opportunity to create in the classroom by completing performance-based tasks or taking more of a role in designing their own learning journey.

These same ideas can be implemented without digital tools and would simply require a common board game or materials that we have in our classroom like paper and dry erase boards. But of course, with all non-technology traditional forms, we can most likely find a digital tool out there that can help us to have the same experience whether or not we are all in the classroom space together when learning. And with digital tools, we can also save time in completing many of these tasks and providing these learning activities to our students.

> **Luis Oliveira, Director of Unified Arts/ELL Teacher, Middletown High School, Rhode Island**
>
> Being comfortable in a collaborative environment is no longer a bonus skill for students. Students will be expected to function in collaborative work environments. Giving our students opportunities to practice the skills that are necessary to be successful collaborative participants falls on teachers. Achieving this with language learners is not an easy task but a required one. I put my students in situations that require them to become collaborative learners. One example is having the students share about their countries. The topic is open-ended and allows students to determine how and what they present. Some students use PowerPoint, others use video or audio. The sharing spaces include Wakelet, Flipgrid or Padlet, and this year will also include Buncee. Using these collaboration spaces not only gives the students voice and choice but it also provides opportunities for classmates to interact and respond to the information provided. This takes it beyond the traditional presentation.

Ide Koulbanis

Using a variety of tools such as Screencastify, Buncee (recording, audio and photo tools) as well as Google Suite tools such as sharing Docs, Slides, and Jamboard . . . there are such a variety of ways to help grow greater communication skills!

Here is a Spanish example that you could use. The Spanish teacher I work with introduced me to Jamboard using this one. The idea is that the students would move the dialogue cards to put them in the correct order. *https://jamboard.google.com/d/1F4zvEpTq6anJ7STxMeT5Pir4wjxcEl_4kf9QSyKbNF0/edit?usp=sharing*

Something else that I should add in that must be a consideration when it comes to communication is making sure that we have a consistent way to communicate with our students. Not just communicating during class about what we are doing, but also being available to answer questions and give feedback. We want to help students to really develop their communicative and interpersonal skills in and out of the classroom. Whether we use an LMS or a messaging app with our classes or rely on email, it's important that students have a way to reach us when they have questions and so we are able to give them feedback. Using a tool like Flipgrid, where we can give video or email feedback, with Buncee we can place comments on their presentation, but there are a lot of other tools that we can bring in to make

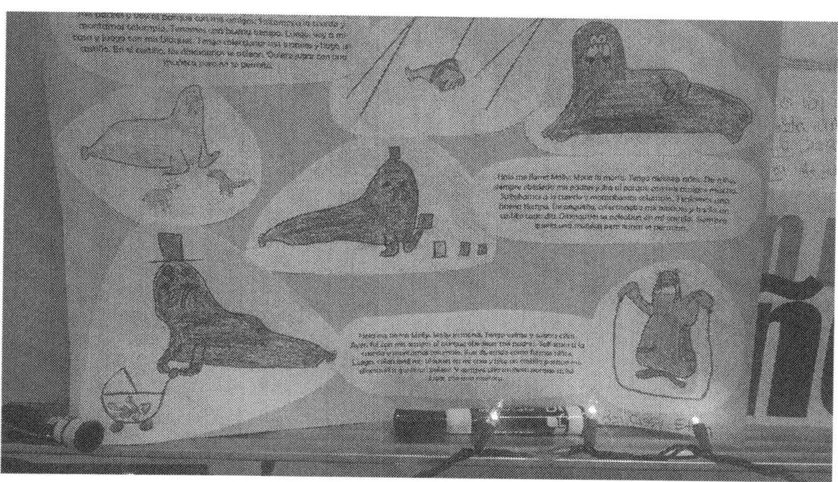

FIGURE 3.9 A collaborative effort to create a story without technology

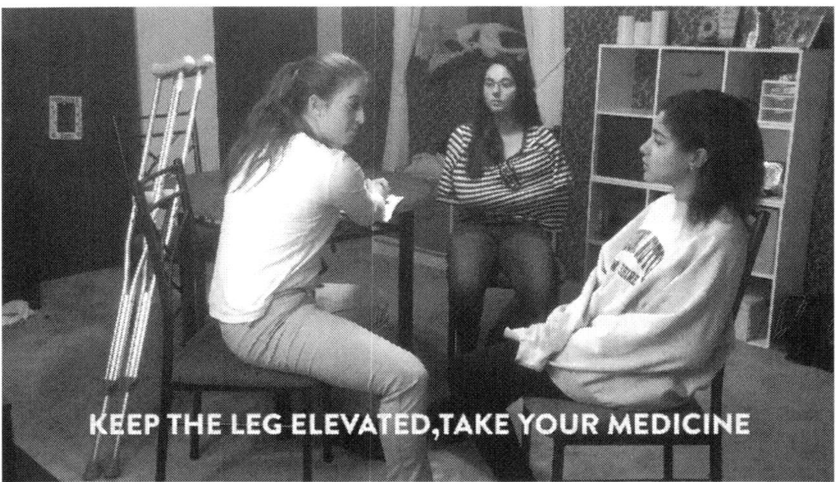

FIGURE 3.10 Screenshot of Spanish III students acting out a medical emergency in a video they created

these even easier. One Google Chrome extension that works very well is *Mote*. With Mote, we can add the extension and then place voice comments into Google Docs and presentations, providing students with authentic, meaningful and timely feedback and also modeling communication skills for them.

Extra Ideas to Explore for Fostering Communication

For students to build their collaborative and communicative skills, have them work in pairs or small groups on a specific task. Give them an opportunity to write a letter, a news article or create an ad for a dream business. One of my favorite activities was having students do skits together in class. Students may choose to act it out live, or some have worked in small groups to create a medical drama with props and special effects. We give students the opportunity to build language skills while tapping into their interests and creativity! The videos and teamwork were phenomenal!

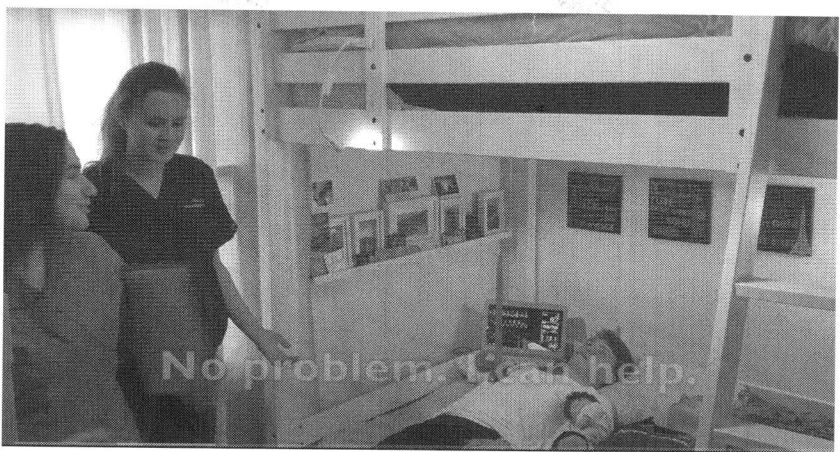

FIGURE 3.11 Screenshot of Spanish III students acting out a medical emergency with props. Spoken in Spanish, they added subtitles

Choose a topic that would be great for a debate in class or provide students with a picture and ask them to come up with their own story about it. Depending on the theme of the unit being studied, perhaps students can create a brochure or poster, design their own game, make a timeline or even build future-ready skills by writing a resume or participating in a mock interview for a job. These are all examples of activities that I have done in my classes over the years and ones which, in most cases, we just relied on what we had on hand in our classroom. However, regardless of whether you are in fully remote or hybrid instruction, these ideas work even if you have not had any interruption with the traditional look of school.

When we design authentic and real-world learning tasks like these, we not only give students the chance to engage in more meaningful learning, be creative and hopefully have fun in the process, these are all tasks which are relevant to our lives. Whether later in education or in our work, having to design a brochure, engage in discussion or take part in an interview, are all tasks that we will encounter at one point or another. Why not give our students the chance to build their language skills while also helping prepare them for what lies ahead in their future, whether in career or college?

4

Breaking Tradition

If You Are Doing This, Then Try This Instead

Chapter Summary

In this chapter you will explore some ideas that may not be considered as traditional in a world language classroom. Whether the ideas are used in STEAM courses or focused on emerging technologies and trends, it is time to take some risks by moving away from the traditional language methods or activities and projects you have been using. The goal is to take something that we are already doing in our classroom and make a slight change, to innovate! Or to try something entirely new and work with our students to learn together. Whether we use tech for the first time or try a different kind of tech, we have the opportunity to be innovative to engage all learners! The ideas will be applicable to in-person and remote learning and provide options for assessments and fun activities to promote student engagement. Try something new like augmented and virtual reality for language learning! Take away quick ideas to get started and be inspired by the educator and student vignettes.

DOI: 10.4324/9781003137665-5

What to expect in this chapter:

- Learn quick ideas to promote collaboration and student engagement
- Explore immersive technologies to use in your classroom
- Gather new tools that work whether in-person, hybrid or fully remote
- Get started with activities and strategies for promoting more active learning

For the first ten years of my teaching career, assessing students involved creating a test or assigning a project. I was using similar methods that my own teachers used and that worked for me when studying French in high school and Spanish in college, and so I transferred those same methods into my own classroom. I took time to write comments on papers and projects and often I would find that many students would not read my comments or take them into consideration and then apply them to their learning. Also, depending on the test that I gave or the project that I assigned, all students received the same questions or the same format that they had to follow. In my classroom, I was the only one leading and making decisions, and I was afraid of my classroom becoming too loud or having students out of their seats. My experience was of a well-structured, teacher-designed and led classroom. However, years ago I realized I needed to give students more choices in how to show what they were learning and to collaborate more with each other. Once I took some risks, I was able to provide more personalized learning experiences, better understand their growth and provide the support and differentiation they needed.

Classes can be made more interesting and engaging today by using the technology available in ways which are beneficial, promote more student autonomy and give students the power of choice. Student empowerment in learning is key. Over the years, I have provided more learning opportunities with choices for the students and have definitely noticed remarkable differences. Because students have choices in what they do, what they share, and how they share it, their learning is personalized and they feel valued. Through these methods, they become more familiar and comfortable with the learning of the target language, leading to increased motivation and engagement in learning.

Beyond supporting their language learning, I also was able to build essential teacher-student relationships in my classroom. By providing more choices, we help students to build their confidence in creating with the language, and it builds their excitement to share their learning with peers. We create opportunities for students to shape their learning and foster the development of student agency through opportunities we create whether through blended instruction and the use of different instructional methods, offering students control in the pace, path, time and place for learning. When we differentiate instruction, it allows us to make adjustments and change the activities to better meet student interests and needs.

First, we need to find some minor changes to start with or some big new ideas to bring into our classrooms. Ask: What are some ideas that we can use that may not require technology but that provide better ways for students to build language skills in and out of our classroom space? Start with some basic activities and mix them up a bit. Bring in the use of social media like Instagram or Snapchat or things like bitmojis, GIFS and memes, to have students create more authentically with the language! My students loved creating #booksnaps with Snapchat to share what they learned from the book we were reading.

Reviewing Vocabulary and Verb Structures

An easy way to get started is to try new ideas when reviewing vocabulary: Bring in social media, have students caption an image, create a meme or leave it up to them! Rather than using traditional worksheets or having students translate text into the target language, do a brainstorm activity to see what they remember and what they can share with others.

Grab paper or create a collaborative whiteboard space using one of the tools mentioned in Chapter 2 and provide them with prompts. Perhaps ask them, "¿Qué recuerdas?" which means "What do you remember?" and prompt them to create with the vocabulary and verbs that they have been studying.

Another idea is to provide a few sentences for students to resequence or to check for grammatical correctness. An activity like this is something I started to do rather than asking students to translate sentences into or from the target language. Translating sentences was something that I did as a student and learned during my student teaching practice, so I kept it as a method used in my own classroom. Now instead, I provide students with sentences that require them to manipulate the word order or focus on making them grammatically correct, which helps them to apply and reinforce their language skills. It also engages them in discussions to share the reasons they made the changes or to apply their learning at a higher level.

With these options, we have the chance to differentiate by providing steps in a process or scaffolded instruction that helps students get started in a more comfortable and individualized way. We can also include sentences in the target language and then provide a word in English that students can then change or translate to help them to build the skills. Providing opportunities for students to engage in interpretive, interpersonal and presentational tasks will provide more personalized learning experiences that engage them in more authentic and meaningful language learning. Choosing the right space or the right tools enables us to provide a lot more than what we could have years ago. However, we always want to focus on the underlying purpose and ask ourselves some questions:

1. Are we helping students to build language skills to achieve a level of proficiency?
2. Do we want them to become more culturally aware and develop SEL skills?
3. Are we focused on promoting more collaboration between students to foster our learning community?
4. Which of these are important not only for language learning and mastery, but essential for students as they prepare for the future?

We need to come up with a quick way to get started that offers a lot of possibilities and then build or add to our toolbox from there, always taking time to reflect and gather student input.

What About the Digital Tools?

When it comes to technology, there are a lot of tools that can help us to do all of these things. We can use our learning management system (LMS) if we have something like Canvas or Schoology, or if we're using Google Classroom or Microsoft Teams. We can use one of the collaborative spaces like Whiteboard.chat or Google Jamboard to provide an opportunity for students to work together even when not in the same physical or virtual learning space. Tools like GoFormative (www.goformative.com) and Nearpod (www.nearpod.com) provide a variety of question types, open-ended responses and other formats to create lessons that we can assign as a student-paced or live lesson. The benefits are that we can keep these collaborations going regardless of the learning space (in-person, hybrid or virtual) and we have access to that real-time data to be better able to support our students as they learn and build skills in the target language, even when we are not together in the classroom.

If we have been in the habit of using different games or activities over the years, we can always make some slight tweaks, whether that means transferring them into the digital space or adding a twist to what the objective is for a game or an activity. Something that has been fun in my classroom especially when doing stations, which was a big change for me, was the use of games for learning. Whether digital games through the game-based learning tools that are available or adapting games from childhood and bringing them into the

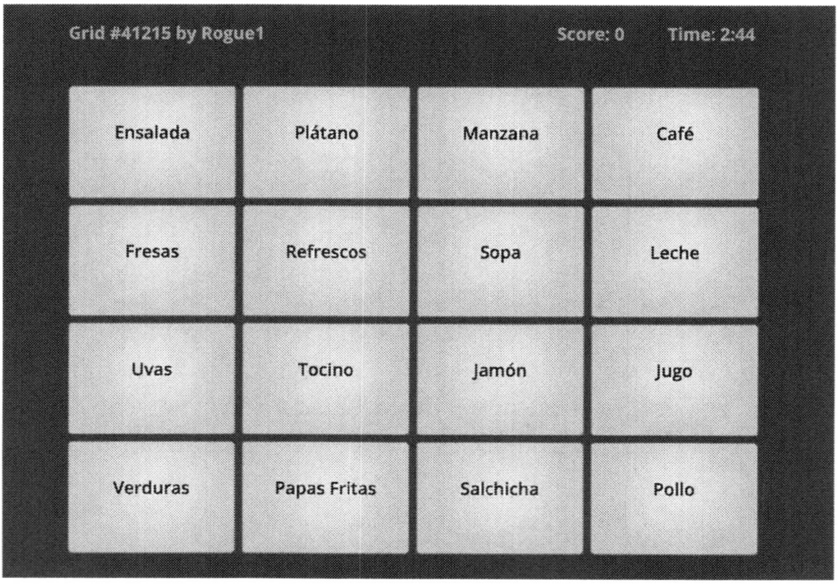

FIGURE 4.1 Puzz Grid game at the beginning

language classroom, we can help students to build their language skills in multiple ways. Educators are creative and can take a concept of a game or even use the game itself and make adjustments as needed so that it fits into the target language or the particular use that we want to try it for. One tool that I found that didn't take much time at all to get started with and ended up being a good way for students to practice vocabulary and verbs was Puzz Grid.

Sometimes I create activities in my class where I give students several categories of words and ask them which one does not fit within the category and why. Other times I use common activities like crosswords, word searches, word scrambles or matching pairs because that repeat interaction with and focusing closely on words leads to better language retention. Each of these activities can be created with paper or note cards in our classroom, but it's also nice to have digital options to create them and to be able to share them with students wherever they are. I've enjoyed Puzz Grid which has the "Connect Four" game theme and requires the player to figure out what the connection is between four of the words in the grid. As you make the connection and click on the "four" correctly, they are then grouped together and moved to the top of the screen. Once all categories are correct, the player can continue the game by trying to figure out the link is between each of the four words in the group. It is a great way to not only help students to remember the vocabulary but also to look at the bigger picture to think about connections between words. We can further the discussion by having students take the words and create a story or write a sentence or ask questions using the verbs and vocabulary. It's just the idea of starting with something a little bit different to hook students into the lesson or to provide some additional practice. Here is an example of a game that I made to introduce it to students. (http://puzzgrid.com/grid/41215). Games can be created for free and sent by email so that you always have the link and can either play it or go back and edit the game as needed.

Using ideas like this are not specific to just language courses but great for any grade level or content area. We can find ways to use activities like this to give students an individual opportunity to interact with the content and process the information in a different way. Especially helpful for visual learners who associate the words or perhaps in this case, start to see a connection and

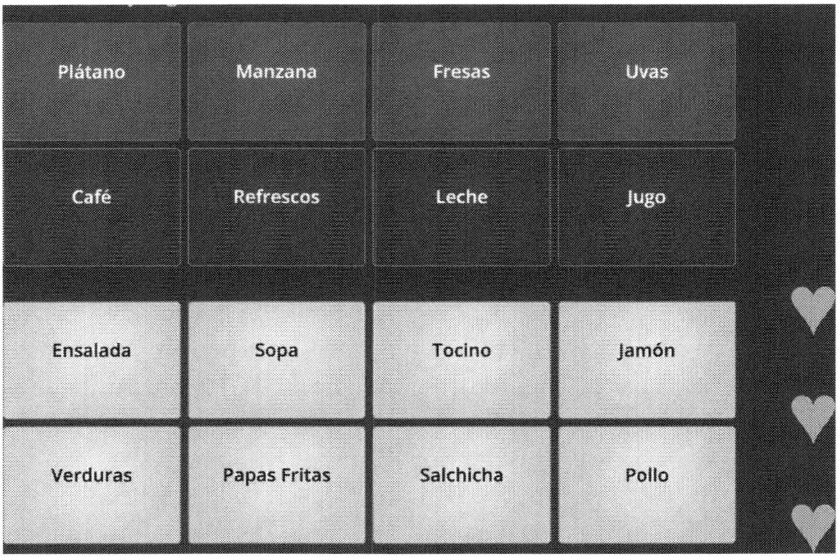

FIGURE 4.2 Puzz Grid game once two sets of categories have been connected

then look more closely at the word choices to find one that fits that category. It goes beyond a simple substitution with the language and asks students to process the information at a higher level. We definitely want to give students as many opportunities to interact with the language but also to then apply it in different ways, whether that be through reading, writing, listening or speaking.

Immersing Students in Learning

For years I have looked for more ways to promote student engagement, especially when I noticed a decrease in my own classroom and reached out to my colleagues and PLN for ideas. I tried some new websites with games and activities for students, which helped, but I knew that I needed to do more. As a STEAM teacher, I had been teaching about augmented and virtual reality and had not thought about using those tools in my Spanish classes. My students have shown me that we definitely need to be open to exploring new ideas in our classroom. And with the recent changes to how we have been providing instruction and as we plan for the future, we need to consider expanding and innovating in the learning space.

Finding ideas that will engage students and spark some curiosity as we shift through in-person, hybrid or fully online learning can sometimes present a challenge. However, when we bring in some of these emerging technologies, we not only increase student engagement but we also help students to build SEL skills as they learn about the world beyond their community. Through augmented and virtual reality tools, we can provide engaging learning experiences for our students that connect them more closely. Student engagement is one area that I have continued to work on over the past few years and especially in our virtual learning environment.

There are hundreds if not thousands of resources to choose from for augmented reality or virtual reality (AR/VR). It can be overwhelming to sort through all of the options or to know where to start. Before exploring the different tools, a good place to start is to consider the purpose for using them. Ask yourself "What can these tools help me to do differently or better for my students?" I try to find tools that have benefits beyond their educational use that will help students to prepare for the future. I look for options that give students a chance to create more with the content and which do not have a big learning curve or time commitment for teachers to get started. When it comes to emerging technologies, we don't need to be a teacher of a STEAM course or have expertise in areas like augmented and virtual reality. With all of the options out there, we can get started rather quickly because of the resources provided within each platform. We just need to choose one or two to get started with in our classrooms and learn with our students. Also, we just need to know enough to get our students started, because then they take it in their own direction and design their own immersive learning experience and create with the language.

As we look for activities and new ideas to keep students engaged, especially as we work through our transitioning learning environments, we have the perfect opportunity to explore emerging technologies like augmented and virtual reality. With traveling around the world or exploring objects up-close being limited, we can implement a few of the AR and VR tools to promote closer exploration and to have students become the creators. By providing students with a chance to more meaningfully engage with the content by moving from consumers to creators, it helps to increase student engagement and leads to higher student achievement. It also enables us to explore difficult-to-see places and to help students become more culturally aware and develop empathy during their learning experiences.

Through the use of these augmented and virtual reality tools, students connect more closely with what they are studying and build upon their knowledge by creating authentic representations of what they have learned. Using these tools goes beyond simply looking at different places; there are more opportunities and choices for student creation and we are better able to meet specific student interests and needs.

Bringing AR/VR to Spanish Class!

For several years when I started with AR/VR, I worked with the students in my eighth-grade STEAM course in the library because it gave us more space to work and all students then had access to a computer. My students were creating their own projects using one of the apps that we had been learning about and were excited at all of the possibilities. During that same time, a study hall was held in the library which had several of the students from my Spanish II class. After a few days, students in Spanish class noticed what the STEAM students were working on asked me why they couldn't "do the cool augmented virtual reality stuff?" I did not have a good answer to that question, nor did I even have an answer. Using augmented and virtual reality was not something that I had thought about using in my Spanish classes other than when we had used Nearpod on a few occasions. Other than that limited experience, I thought that AR/VR was a topic that was only relevant to the STEAM course on emerging technology that I had been teaching. Although I had used Nearpod for its virtual field trips in my class, the VR tours were something that students would simply consume but not create. After I was asked that question from my students, I gave some AR/VR a try in my Spanish II class to see how it would work.

Getting Started With AR/VR

It just so happened to be towards the end of the school year and student engagement had been down following a spring period of testing, sports and other activities that filled the schedules and drained energy. We were trying to keep pushing through to the end of the year as we also were preparing for final exam review. It seemed like the perfect time to try something innovative and that might just help to boost student engagement. I always enjoy trying new ideas in the spring and at the end of the school year so that I have time to consider the benefits and reflect over the summer in preparation for the new school year.

Getting started with something like augmented and virtual reality might seem to be a difficult concept to tackle at first, but it doesn't need to be. There are enough options available that make it easy to get started and help us to make a connection to the content that we are teaching. AR/VR is a topic we can all bring into our classrooms to provide different and more immersive experiences for students, especially as we are working through transitioning learning environments. There are a lot of choices out there, and we just need to find a few to get started with. Students can create with the language using these emerging technologies, which will not only empower them through authentic and meaningful learning experiences, but will offer more active learning and help to prepare them for the future by learning about technologies that likely will become part of the workplace and the future of education.

You might wonder where to start with so many possibilities out there. Because I love learning so much and enjoy gathering as many resources as I can and trying some in my STEAM classes and also in my Spanish classes, I have multiple lists that would be great for you to start with. Remember that you don't have to be the expert, you only need to know enough to get started and then give the students a chance to explore and then create on their own. For a long time, I thought that I had to be the expert with any method or tool that I brought into my classroom, for fear of not knowing the answer to a question from one of my students. However, I soon realized that there are three important things to keep in mind that benefit us and our students:

First, we can't possibly know all of the answers.

Second, it is important for us to serve as models for our students that learning is a lifelong process and we are always learning,

And third, we show students that it is important to take risks with learning, whether trying new things or risking being wrong. When we show that it is okay to not know an answer and to ask others for help – or even better, ask students to help us – it goes a long way to building confidence and comfort in the classroom and the learning process.

Since the students that asked me "Why don't we do the cool things?" were in my Spanish II class, I decided to give the AR/VR experience a try in their class first. We had been working on narrating in the past tense and students were having some trouble with deciding which past tense to use in Spanish. It has always been a grammar point that students struggle with each year as they try to learn the difference between the two past tenses in Spanish, the preterit and the imperfect. The vocabulary unit focuses on narrating about one's childhood or retelling an event, and I find that the more personalized students make their stories, the easier it is to distinguish between the two. In this unit, I spend a lot of time telling fairy tales and demonstrating actions in the classroom or asking students to talk about their weekend or recent activities that they participated in to help them better distinguish between the two past tenses. However, it is always me doing the demonstrations or creating the examples. I thought that creating with augmented and virtual reality and working collaboratively to create a story with classmates would help students to build their skills and lead to better retention of the content in a more meaningful way.

We spent about two weeks working on their projects, and while I was providing some feedback, students were taking the lead more and helping their classmates in their own groups and in the class as a whole. Being able to explore their own AR and VR world and those created by their peers made a big difference in the content retention for all students. As they included the vocabulary, specific people and objects into new virtual spaces, their engagement in learning increased and their confidence in using the verb tenses to narrate improved. Even during the following year when students were asked about the verb tenses or their vocabulary from that chapter, they remembered it better than in previous classes. Because of the hands-on, more interactive and immersive experience that they had to create with the language in those virtual spaces, student retention of the material was much greater.

Here are some options to get started with in your classroom and that will work for any level or language. The first one, CoSpaces Edu, the one I used with my Spanish II class, is a good one to start with. These can be great for simple assessments or creating some performance assessments for your students in your language courses.

1. CoSpaces Edu is a virtual reality platform that I have used many years and which is a favorite of my eighth grade students each year. While virtually teaching my STEAM Emerging Technology course was initially a little more challenging during the 2020–21 school year, using tools like CoSpaces Edu provides students with the chance to learn about emerging technologies and collaborate with classmates regardless of where they are. It was a lot of fun to teach the students in Spanish II about augmented and virtual reality and give them time to create with the language using something different than anything they had ever used before. Teachers who are nervous about getting started don't have to worry as there are ready-made templates and lesson plans available to choose from that can be used and adapted for language classrooms. Students will find what they need by exploring the library full of characters, animals, objects, transportation, different environments and more that will enable language learners to create meaningful work using their vocabulary.

When I started with my Spanish II class, I was not entirely sure what to do, so I thought quickly and decided to have students create a story about their childhood. I was a little bit nervous about trying it at first, wondering if students would follow the project guidelines. Would they figure out how to use the platform and would it be beneficial? I knew that I would be there to provide guidance or redirection as needed, and that even though I may not have all of the answers, it would be a beneficial and meaningful learning experience for me as well as for my students.

As with other projects, I tried to be quite flexible with specific requirements. What I typically do is provide an overview of specific verb tenses or vocabulary that students need to include but then leave it open for them to explore and create on their own. Beyond creating a scene and adding in relevant vocabulary and verb tenses using text and speech boxes, they could also record and upload audio in their project, which helped to develop speaking skills too. Another benefit is for students to be able to work together on a team, continuing to build SEL skills and becoming more comfortable and confident in language learning together with peers.

Especially for remote learning environments, being able to have students work together using a tool like CoSpaces Edu makes a difference in their learning. Whether they create a space

FIGURE 4.3 Students collaborating on a CoSpaces Edu project in Spanish II

in 360, design a Spanish or language-themed parkour game, collaborate on writing an interactive story or retell a story they have read in class, students will enjoy creating in VR as a way to develop their language skills. Once all groups create their projects, it's fun to share them and give students the opportunity to explore the other creations in augmented and virtual reality. A more immersive language-learning experience that students will retain and connect more with.

2. Devar: Depending on the grade level you teach and of course making sure students have access to devices, there are a lot of AR and VR apps which are fun to use for a twist on traditional digital storytelling tools. Devar is an app that offers several lively characters with animations that can be brought into the classroom or home environment and be an engaging way to get students creating more with the language. If we want to boost creativity and imagination, we can ask students to choose one of the characters to narrate a story.

   Getting started with Devar is easy and it is another fun way for students and teachers to learn more about augmented reality while practicing target language skills. With the different choices in Devar characters, students can create a story solely based on imagination by connecting it with a specific theme or vocabulary unit, narrating childhood or writing a children's book or fairy tale are always good ideas to start with. Bringing in tools like this are also a fun way to review material in preparation for an assessment or even the end of the year exam. There are many possibilities when it comes to these tools, we just need to start with one. Devar provides another great choice for digital storytelling and can be a unique way to get to learn more about student progress with the language too! It can also be fun for teachers to create a welcome message for students at the start of the school year, make a fun introduction to the class or to explain a grammar topic or introduce vocabulary using a tool like Devar. What better way to engage students or spark curiosity for language learning by giving students the chance to create something in AR and VR!

3. Figment AR is one of my all-time favorite apps because of what you can do with it. When I first started to explore the app, I created some fun scenes in my house, in my neighborhood and even one time on the beach. What I realized is that we don't need a specific "space" to be able to use apps like this. No matter what vocabulary or verbs we might be covering in our language classes, we can encourage students to explore the space around them or to adventure out into their community and create something fun to apply their language skills.

To start, think about the different vocabulary and verb topics that you cover in your classes, especially the ones that tend to be more challenging for students to retain or that you might be in need of a new idea to spark student engagement. Offer students the opportunity to share their learning by using the Figment AR app to narrate their own story. My students have used it for creating short stories that have animated characters and special effects like snow or fireworks. Some topics we cover that this would work well for are talking about childhood traditions and family activities. These added elements really help students to create with the relevant language terms in a space that promotes creativity. Not only is Figment for AR, it also transforms into VR through the use of "portals" that can be added into your experience. A fun element is when students add in portals, moving them from AR to VR, which results in them getting "trapped" inside of the portals that they create! Although they're not really trapped but simply need to find the portal back into the real world, it presents an opportunity for students to figure out how to express that they are lost or to ask for directions. It is always good to continue to review prior vocabulary and work on negotiating meaning during what might be unexpected situations.

FIGURE 4.4 Figment AR, possibilities with characters and portals to create a story!

For Some Additional Ideas, Try These

- Ask students to add portals and then once inside the portal, narrate in the target language what they see.
- Ask students to pretend they are giving a tour of their town and create a short video using the app.
- Create a walking tour of the school or follow a typical class schedule and use the scene to generate a conversation with a classmate.
- Make up a pretend trip or adventure using the characters, portals and special effects in the app. Get students talking about what they did on the trip or describing a location and talking about the buildings and the people that they see in that space.

There are a lot of possibilities, and like I said before, we don't have to know everything that there is about each tool, we just need to know enough to get our students started. While we want our students to be the creators, it's also important that we continue to create right along with them. What can you create and share? How about designing a welcome to your classroom or introducing a unit by creating your own Figment AR experience to share with students?

4. Merge EDU: Imagine holding a frog, a volcano, the earth, statues and more for close explorations right in your hands! Merge EDU is an AR/VR platform that provides more interactive learning for students to explore science-related topics in AR through Merge Explorer. Merge EDU has Immersive Reader, which means that students can also listen to the language being spoken to describe what they are seeing, or students can simply use one of the options to create a scene and narrate it in the target language. Perhaps do a cross-curricular collaboration with a science or art teacher and engage students in learning about the other content area and applying their target language skills in different areas. For educators looking to try the full EDU version, there is a free lesson called "Terraforming Earth" to learn more about the lesson

components and see the layers of the earth. Again, it can be added into a language classroom because of the Immersive Reader. I would recommend a cross-curricular collaboration or perhaps asking students to complete the lesson and then providing them with a performance task.

One of my favorite features of Merge is using Object Viewer, which has numerous collections of objects and scenes that would be great for having students create a space in AR to narrate! For example, choosing the architecture collection, you can find famous structures from countries around the world. Choose from the Eiffel Tower, Easter Island, Kokura Castle, Mesoamerican pyramid or a Chinese pagoda, to name a few. With these options, students could use the app to create a city in their space and record a narration in the target language. There are several additional categories that would work including Garden, for describing fruits and vegetables, Museum to create an art exhibit, or one of the animal collections to design a zoo or for making another creative story! With the app, students can bring their creations into the real world and continue to build language skills in more innovative and engaging ways.

5. Nearpod: I have mentioned Nearpod several times throughout the book because it offers so many possibilities for use in our language classrooms. From helping students to develop SEL skills, explore and share for PBL to providing interactive lessons for students so they feel more connected during hybrid or virtual learning, are all reasons that I have continued to keep it in my toolkit. However, the reason that I started to use it was because I was working on my master's degree and had to complete a group Nearpod lesson project. It piqued my interest and so I then created my first lesson for my students in Spanish III, which gave them more of an immersive experience as they learned about South America. Rather than simply looking at pictures in the book or watching videos or listening to me describe some

FIGURE 4.5 Merge EDU location choices to create with object viewer

of the places we were reading about, it put the learning right in their hands.

Nearpod provides many options for promoting student engagement through its interactive multimedia platform. My initial exploration of using VR in my Spanish classes was with Nearpod. At first, I thought it would be limited to using it only when we were reading about different places where Spanish was spoken, so I could give my students a closer look and to promote some curiosity and definitely some discussion. When I started using it, I thought that I needed to create all of the lessons myself, however I learned that I did not have to be the only one creating. Depending on the age of your students, they can also create lessons. For all teachers, there are thousands of ready-to-run lessons to choose from, which include 3D objects to explore and VR field trips in addition to all of the other activities we can add to a Nearpod lesson.

Using Nearpod is great for immersing students in different learning experiences or "traveling," especially during hybrid or distance learning. It is a great tool for assessing students and creating more interactive and engaging lessons that spark curiosity! Using virtual reality as a hook into a lesson definitely makes a difference for students and can be a way to promote more conversation in the target language between students whether in the classroom or in a virtual environment. Nearpod also has the Immersive Reader, so students can take advantage of that feature to listen to the pronunciation and to translate text into the target language, which provides another way to engage with the language they are learning. Get started by exploring the Spanish lessons focused on grammar topics or cultural themes and then add in some VR trips and additional activities and make it your own.

5. Thyng App: A personal favorite for creating augmented reality experiences that include animated characters, text, GIFS and more to inspire creative storytelling with the target language. You can even upload your own 3D objects or videos into the Thyng App and submit your

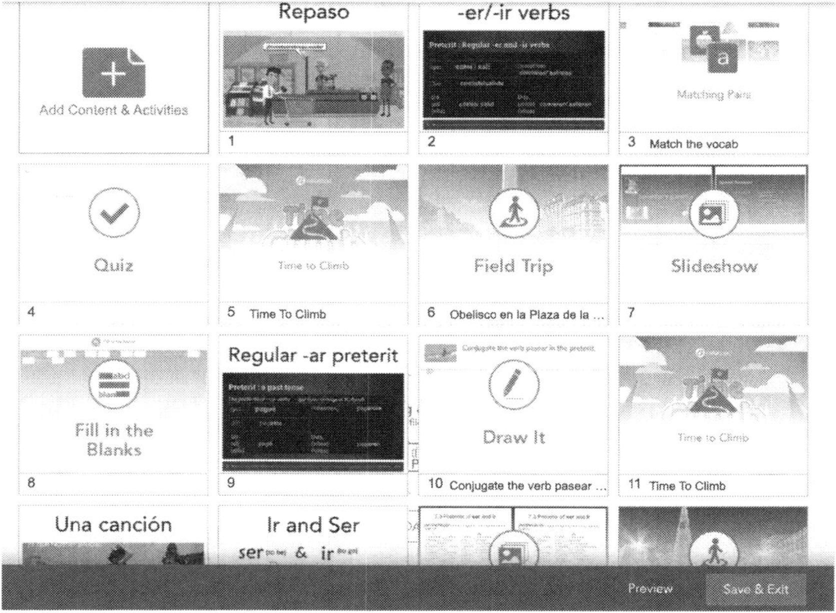

FIGURE 4.6 Nearpod lesson for Spanish I example activities

"Thyngs" to be included in their library for anyone to scan and experience! Thyng can also be used to scan a target image and record up to a ten-second video to go with your target image. It is available on iOS and Android and is free!

Here Are Three Ideas to Try With Your Class

- Have students read a short story or a poem and use the book or poem as the target image, meaning when the object is scanned, it is what triggers the AR experience or recording. Students can then choose from the animations and characters available to add in the background or interacting with the book, and then record themselves speaking in the target language to summarize what they have read or retell a story.
- Provide students with a theme or a prompt like describing their house or talking about a favorite food, for a few ideas.

Have students create an AR experience to add to it with their description in the target language.

- Encourage students to get outside and describe something in nature or a favorite place in their community and add animations and a narration to it.

These are just a few authentic, meaningful and definitely more engaging learning opportunities for students to explore. From

FIGURE 4.7 Thyng app for using target image and adding in effects and audio

what I have experienced, students will retain the content better because they are making the choice in what to create and they become more curious about learning. They are also building their skills in a way that is more personalized and more impactful for their learning.

When Do We Need Technology?

We know that it is not always about the technology, even though there are so many options out there that enable us to provide more for our students and for ourselves when it comes to learning. It is always important to think about the underlying purpose, the "why" for choosing a specific digital tool or even a teaching method in our classroom. How can we create the best opportunities that will enable our students to build skills in the target language in authentic, personalized and purposeful ways? When we can bring in some exciting ideas that not only challenge our students to create using different technologies but keep us learning right with and definitely from them, it promotes a more supportive and welcoming classroom culture for learning. We model the importance of lifelong learning and of taking risks with new ideas and enjoying the process of learning itself.

Providing Choices

It is important to offer multiple options to students that lead to more meaningful experiences that promote the development of essential skills for the future and empower them through self-driven learning. While some typical activities that we might engage our students in like field trips or travel abroad might be more challenging during certain times, whether due to the financial cost or perhaps as a result of situations such as the pandemic, we have options available to us now through emerging technologies that we can leverage. Wanting to take students on field trips or imagine what a place or a thing might look like up close is now possible with so many new technologies and in particular, the immersive tools for augmented reality (AR) and virtual reality (VR). When we offer these options, we create more interactive learning experiences for our students and add some extra fun into the learning experience!

We can use these tools to empower students to create with the language in unique ways. Using some of these AR/VR options would be good choices for having students complete some performance-based assessments and would infuse some creativity, critical thinking and perhaps even problem-solving into their language learning journey.

There are many tools available specific to augmented and virtual reality, and while they may not have a direct correlation to the language that we teach, we can always find a way to make it work. A few years ago, I tried using a virtual speech app in my Spanish IV class. Essentially it is an app that enables people to practice giving speeches or to experience a simulated job interview in front of a variety of well-known companies or organizations. I had my Spanish IV students, who were studying vocabulary related to career exploration and travel, prepare to do an interview using this app with a partner. Prior to that experience, Spanish IV students created a cover letter and resume and did a mock interview in class with a classmate. This experience was great preparation for the future, while of course giving them language practice that was meaningful and relevant. It didn't involve any technology other than searching for a job to apply for and creating the resume and cover letter. The objective was for students to apply for a job in a Spanish-speaking country, prepare a cover letter and resume and then have an interview. It was a really great experience and I still have some of the examples that students created. Having the Virtual Speech app option just takes it to a different level. For a few ideas, students could upload a speech or other document and practice responding to questions in a simulated interview. Students could prepare for a presentation by practicing in the app with an audience and build confidence. It could just present a different option that sparks curiosity and engages students more in presenting an idea.

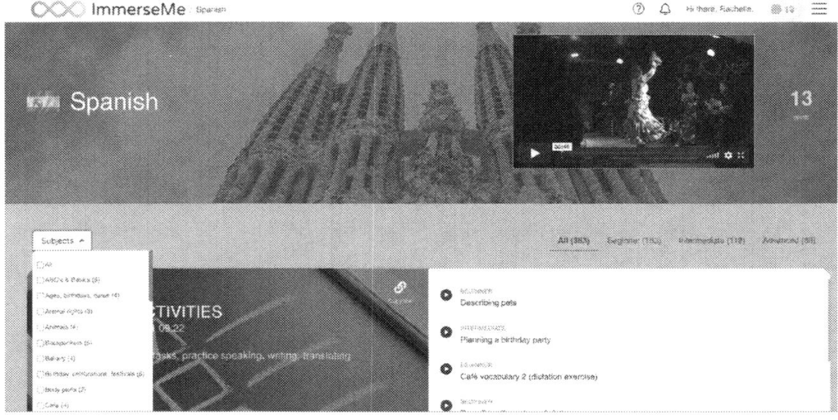

FIGURE 4.8 ImmerseMe dashboard options for lessons and topics

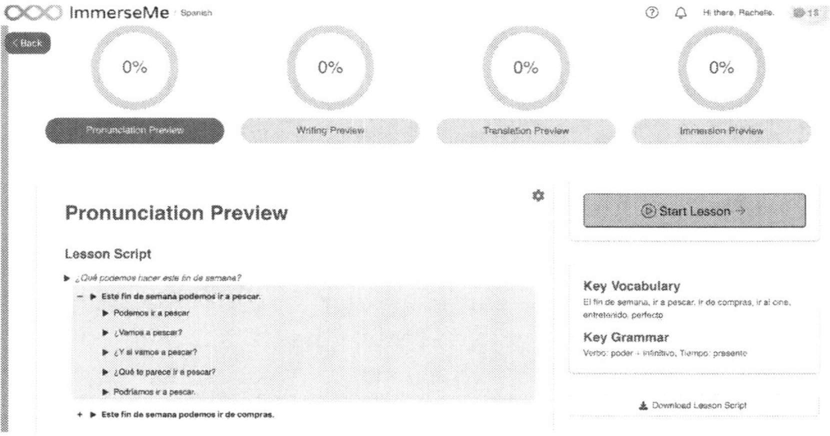

FIGURE 4.9 ImmerseMe tasks including lesson script and resources

Another wonderful language tool that I learned about which offers a truly immersive language-learning experience in virtual reality for students is ImmerseMe. ImmerseMe is a virtual reality language learning platform that offers nine different languages and includes more than 3,000 different interactive experiences. Teachers have an account with a dashboard for students, and students can work through a

Jimena Licitra: From traditional to transformational!

These are three examples on how to transform a traditional activity from a textbook into an inspiring activity/project.

1. This is an image of the textbook I was supposed to use with my Year 9 students.
2. For this second example, I had to cover recipes vocabulary. My main objective was for students to learn vocabulary and improve their reading comprehension of recipes in German. The textbook activity had the images of cooking tools, the recipe, steps in the process and additional information for preparing the dish. However, instead of doing this, I created a Quizlet with recipes and cooking vocabulary. We then created a German Christmas book with traditional recipes together. I collected the recipes in a Wakelet (www.wakelet.com) collection and provided students with it, the Quizlet and with clear instructions on how to do their recipes with simple sentences. Students had to read the original recipes and simplify them to create our book. We used three class sessions for this, and student engagement was 100% guaranteed. Some students even got together to cook their recipe (see Figure 4.12) and sent me their videos. Here you can see an example:
3. My third suggestion for breaking tradition is simply using Mentimeter.com to review the unit with your students. You can ask students for vocabulary words or a response to a question and then have it generate a word cloud.

variety of tasks and activities focused on translation, dictation, and immersion. With ImmerseMe, students experience real-world interactions such as eating in a restaurant, shopping, exploring and traveling and more authentic opportunities to build language skills in a space that is comfortable for them and helps students to build their confidence.

In each topic, there are multiple ways for students and educators to practice. Each activity comes with the lesson script and pronunciation preview which includes some prompts. There are also key vocabulary words and grammar points included. Students have really enjoyed using this immersive language experience in our classes!

Instead of using the book activity, I created a collaborative wall and we worked together on gathering ideas. The kids loved the interaction. We used the tool *https://slice.wbrain.me/* to create the board.

c Vorteile und Nachteile – Sammelt an der Tafel.

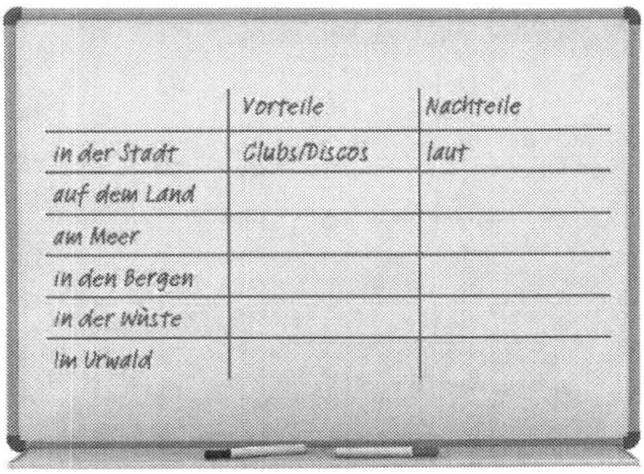

	Vorteile	Nachteile
in der Stadt	Clubs/Discos	laut
auf dem Land		
am Meer		
in den Bergen		
in der Wüste		
im Urwald		

FIGURE 4.10 Image of text activity used before changing to a more collaborative activity

Taking a Risk and Breaking Tradition

There have been a lot of different ideas shared in this chapter, some which require technology and others which simply require a slight shift in what we are doing or the traditional materials we are using. The best advice I can offer is to start by trying to find one interesting and more engaging activity or experience that promotes student choice and voice in learning and which will empower students to take more of the lead in the classroom.

Making the initial shift from the way we have been teaching or the comfortable or traditional methods we have been using can be difficult, but we have an opportunity and perhaps the push that we have needed, to do something different and innovative. The changes in our instruction and the look of school have not been under ideal circumstances by any means, but we should take advantage of the opportunity to try something different and maybe even scary at first. It just takes one slight change to start making a big difference for our students and ourselves.

Our goal is to prepare students so that regardless of what they decide to do after leaving our classrooms, they will be ready with the right skills and real-world awareness they need to be successful in a constantly evolving world.

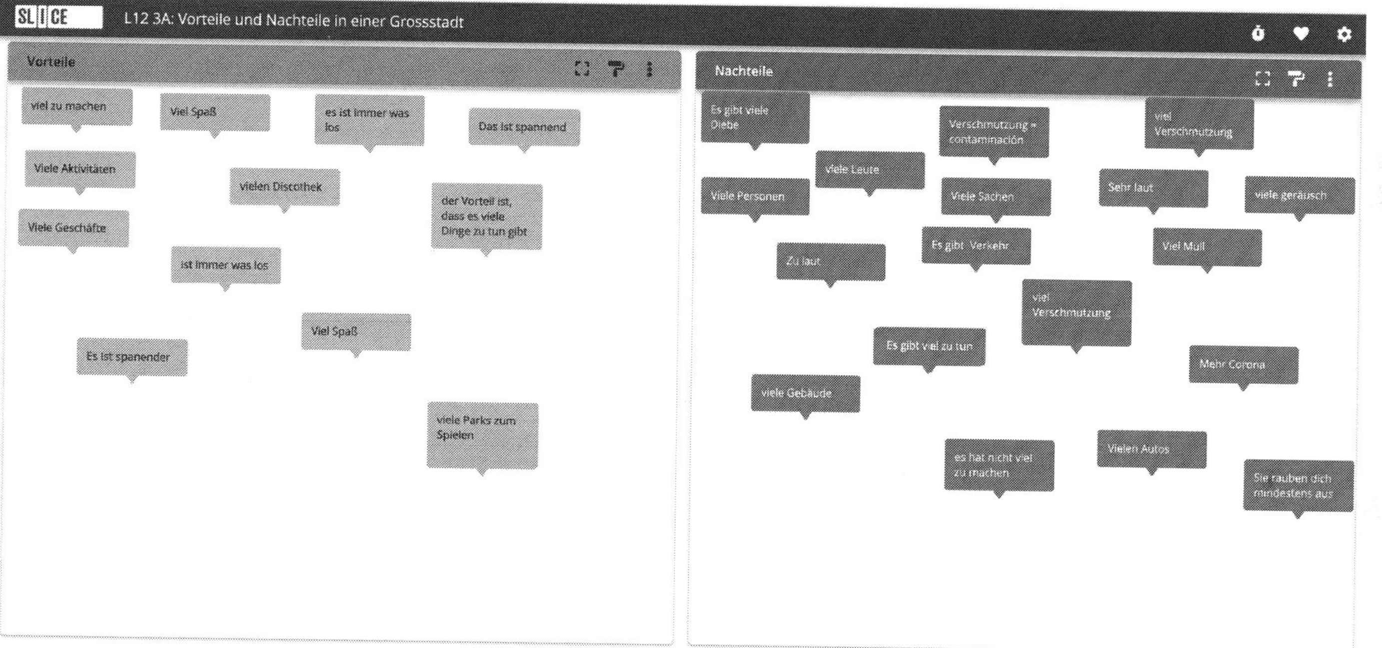

FIGURE 4.11 Slice, a collaborative wall used for gathering ideas

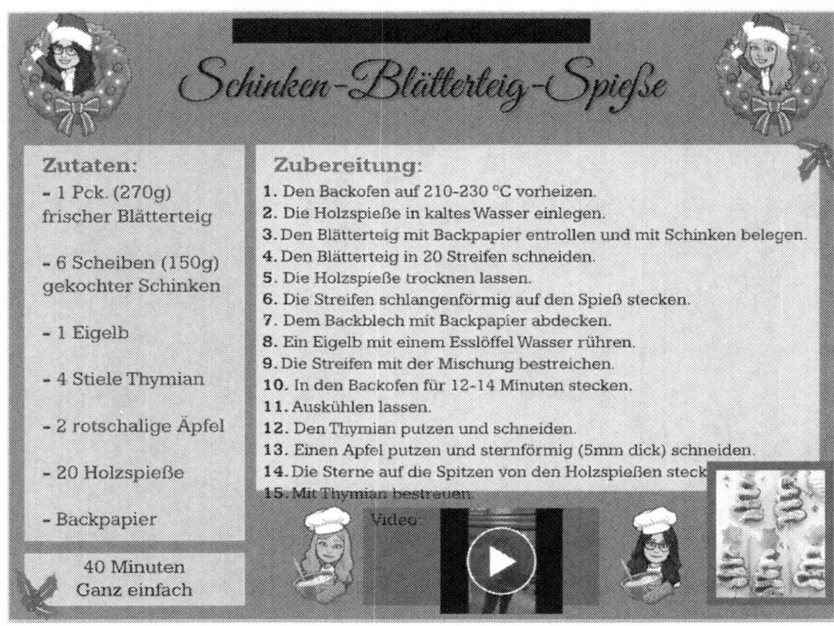

FIGURE 4.12 Activity completed instead of the textbook recipe, a graphic with student video

5

Student-Led Classrooms

Stepping Aside and Letting Students Learn and Lead

Chapter Summary

In this chapter, you will learn many ideas for promoting student choice and voice by having students decide how to show their learning, whether through the use of digital tools or by designing their own demonstration of learning, with or without the need for technology. I will share how I started to encourage students to explore their own unique interests and engage in more personalized and student-driven learning activities that enable them to develop their voice in learning. We will explore how to move students from consumers to instead become creators and leaders in the classroom. While it can feel uncomfortable at first to give up some control in the classroom and step aside, the benefits are tremendous for student learning. Some of the ideas shared will include project-based learning, genius hour, student choice boards, HyperDocs and more options that are focused on having students in the lead. The methods and tools will be applicable to in-person and remote learning and provide a variety of quick ideas to help students develop their language skills and build confidence to take the lead more.

DOI: 10.4324/9781003137665-6

What to expect in this chapter:

- Ideas to get started with more student-driven learning
- Tools that promote collaboration and empower learners to lead
- Strategies for any learning space!

How to Make the Shift

We know that making changes like this can feel uncomfortable, shifting from our common practices can feel and look chaotic at times. When I made changes in my classroom, I worried about it looking unstructured and as though I did not have control. However, I learned that doing things differently and being more flexible in planning can lead to more authentic and meaningful conditions for learning, not just for students but for us too. Students will engage more and thrive in learning environments that are fueled by choice, that embrace risk-taking and provide opportunities that push them to apply their skills in innovative ways.

A few years ago, I noticed changes in student engagement in my classroom. I felt as though I was not reaching my students and that I was doing too much of the decision making with little room for student input. I was the one creating all materials, speaking for the class, deciding the ways for students to show learning. It took a shift in my mindset and some rearranging of furniture in my classroom to make some big changes that truly made a difference for my students and helped me to continue making changes and taking risks. If we seize the opportunity to try new things and continue to grow, we will better provide our best selves for those we lead and learn with. The time to do this is now. We have a chance to try new ideas and continue to explore by connecting with other educators and learning from our shared experiences. To do the best for our students, we must create learning experiences that provide more for them than simply a way to practice the target language. We must aim for authentic, purposeful learning experiences that promote student engagement and increase motivation, foster creativity in learning, encourage some risk-taking with an added benefit being the building of relationships and a positive and welcoming classroom culture.

How Can We Place Students in the Lead More?

A few years ago, whenever I changed the structure of my room to get rid of the rows and instead create stations, there was an in-between period of time where I wasn't really sure what I was doing with my classroom setup. I knew that I wanted to do less of the talking and give students more of an opportunity to take the lead in the classroom. I didn't want to stay in the front of the class the whole time and continue to feel disconnected from the students and have them feel disconnected from one another. However, I wasn't sure of the best way to go about making changes. I was also mindful of students who might be uncomfortable with taking the lead or speaking up in front of their classmates. One thing that I was sure of is when students can work with a partner or in small groups, it goes a long way to helping them to become more comfortable in the learning space and to build their confidence in the classroom. As leaders, we need to become more comfortable with taking some risks and do more ourselves.

In 2015, I started to challenge myself more by applying to speak at local language and EdTech conferences to share what we were doing in our classroom. I was teaching French and Spanish at the time and found an opportunity to take students to PETE&C (Pennsylvania Educational Technology Expo and Conference), held in Hershey, PA, to participate in the student technology showcase. Based on my observations in the classroom, when it came to students creating presentations or making their own games, their excitement about that experience and how comfortable they were talking about it, I believed that having them share that with other teachers and students would be a great opportunity. It would be beneficial for them to share their excitement for language learning and to inform others about the benefits of technology in all classrooms. And maybe the biggest benefit was that it gave them a chance to build their leadership and collaborative skills in and out of the classroom. During that first conference experience with students presenting, I noticed how engaged they were in sharing their work with attendees and supporting one another as they presented. They learned so much from one another, not just about the different digital tools they used, but how they engaged more in the language by exploring all of their creations. That first

FIGURE 5.1 Our final presentations together at PETE&C after four years

experience led me to think about how I might create similar opportunities for all students that wouldn't necessarily require traveling to a conference to do so. As educators, how can we involve students more in making their decisions about how to show what they are learning and involve them more in teaching classmates or other educators about what is working for them in the classroom?

Sharing What You Know

A few years ago, when I noticed a decrease in student engagement, it led me to take a closer look at the way I was teaching and interacting in my classroom. I thought about the materials that I was using, the assignments I was giving, the assessments that I was creating and the projects that I was designing for my students. I looked at my classroom space and considered how I might make some changes that would make a big impact on student learning and building relationships in the classroom. My class was very structured with every minute being accounted for and covered by me. I was providing all instruction and content for students, leaving little time for their input on most days. Again, I had developed my teaching methods by basing them off of the ones that I was familiar with as a student in high school and college and by comparing it to my student teaching experiences. I thought that my classroom teaching style and materials had to reflect the other classrooms and had not previously considered breaking any type of traditional classroom setup or format.

My mindset changed one day when I decided that I needed something to be different. All it took was for me to remove the desks from the rows one morning a few minutes before class. Not completely sure of what to do with the new setup, I got through that day by asking students for their feedback and definitely winging it for most of the day. From that day on, I started to explore different ideas that I had read about or heard about from other educators but never considered using in my own classroom. As a language teacher, many of the ideas that I had heard of didn't seem like ones that I could bring into my classroom. Either they involved a digital tool that I didn't see a clear connection to language learning or they were concepts or strategies that seemed like a lot to take on and I wasn't sure that I could do it. I looked for ways to help students become more independent and have more personalized and meaningful learning opportunities. To do so means that we need to have less of a presence and be there more to facilitate rather than to be the only one leading and talking in the classroom. We can learn from our students as well as teach them. There needs to be a shift in leadership in our classrooms, and it is time that we start exploring new ideas and taking some risks.

New Opportunities

Because I had suddenly changed the layout of my room and wasn't really sure what to do with it, some things that I tried kind of just happened or fell into place. After my experience with students at the student showcase where they took turns sharing ideas with one another, I thought I should try that in my classroom. One of the first ideas that I tried was having students come to class with a lesson to teach one of their classmates. The desks were set up in pairs and I assigned the student on one side of the desk to be the teacher and the other was the student. If we were learning verb conjugations or new vocabulary themes, the homework was for the "teacher" in each pair to create an activity for class the next day. I was impressed right away. During that first experiment, students came into class with a worksheet that they made, a video that they found or a game that they created. For their homework, they had a choice and took the time to create and have fun learning in a way that was more interesting to them and that offered the chance to build their skills in a more meaningful way. It also helped them to build confidence in the classroom by building their skills in a comfortable space with one peer and then expanding to leading a class lesson. I learned so many new ideas from the students, which pushed me to explore other changes that I could make in what I was doing or what had been tradition in my classroom.

To design a "teacher for a day" activity such as the one that I did, first think about the content that you cover. I tend to select from topics that have been challenging for students or ones which I am hoping to gather some new ideas for my own practice. When it comes to verbs for example, there are a lot of different activities that we can do with our students to help them build confidence in conjugating verbs or knowing how to narrate in different tenses for example. However, when we create these types of opportunities, students have more control, design their own learning path and it reinforces their learning as they teach and interact with their class partner. When we reverse those roles, we also provide reinforcement of the lesson because the students take turns teaching each other. A "teacher for a day" activity is not only beneficial for building language skills but social emotional learning skills too, as students learn to interact with their peers and provide support as they set their own goals for learning. This is also a way to provide differentiation in the classroom by learning from the choices of our students and then giving them a way to share and show learning.

Where to begin? Perhaps start with a specific verb tense or type, a vocabulary unit, a cultural topic or even leave the choice up to the students. It may be a bit uncomfortable for students at first because they are accustomed to doing the activities that we create and looking to us for direction. However, by supporting them as they design and teach the lesson to their peers, we promote collaboration, creativity and SEL skills and empower students as leaders and creators in our classrooms.

Another way to do this is either at the beginning of the year or at points where you want to do a cumulative review. Over the summer, we are to give assignments to students to complete in preparation for the next school year, whether it be for an AP course or the next level of the language being studied. What I have done instead is provide a reader and also give students the chance to lead a lesson of their own.

At the start of each school year, students from prior levels of Spanish return with a lesson to teach their classmates that will help to review the content from the year prior. For many years, I was the one doing all of the review and after having done the teacher for a day activity in my Spanish II classes originally, I decided that perhaps I needed to branch out a bit. Rather than assign some worksheets or other specific activities during the summer, I would offer students a choice in a book to read at their own pace and some options for creating a lesson to teach for review in our classroom. Again, it's not something that requires technology, as students can create worksheets or some other visual presentation to do in class. However, with many schools being in hybrid or fully virtual learning, or potentially having to make those shifts in the future, we also need to help students to explore some of the digital options out there. Many of the most common tools have been mentioned in prior chapters and can be great choices, but there were a few times that my students surprised me. I remember students who came to class to present or emailed a link to a presentation created with tools like Buncee, GoFormative, Kahoot!, Nearpod, Quizizz and Padlet. It had not occurred to me that students would use some of the tools that had been part of our classroom and which were teacher-created. Students took it to another level and made their own lessons to teach classmates. Their comfort with the content and choice in how to teach a lesson pushed them to take more of a lead. It not only reinforced their own understanding in a more authentic way, but it provided a much more authentic way to connect with their classmates.

The best way to get started is to just give it a go in one of your courses; create a space, whether that's in the classroom or in a digital space, for students to collaborate. Perhaps in a breakout room and giving students a chance to share their screen or do an activity with the others in their small group. It builds comfort and confidence in that space. There are a lot of possibilities and definitely a lot of benefits to having students be the teachers for a day or more!

Student-Driven Learning Options

Once I noticed the benefits of having students come up with their own ideas or choose how to practice what they were learning, I decided to explore more ways to open up additional choices for students. I decided to give choice boards a try. With only minimal knowledge of what they actually were and how to use them, I took a chance with using them in my classroom. What I have noticed about myself over the past few years is that I am more willing to try something spontaneously and hope that it works as I plan, but ready to accept if it doesn't go well and just keep going. To create my first choice board, I grabbed a piece of paper and quickly drew a tic-tac-toe board and tried to think of nine options for students to spend the class time practicing Spanish. The choices were quite different from our usual learning activities. Options included drawing a picture, making flashcards, writing short stories, or making up a game using one of the game-based learning tools that we have been using, such as Kahoot! or Quizizz. The choice board didn't take long to create, just a few minutes to write it down quickly and make some copies for class. Initially my students were not that impressed, confused by the handwriting on the paper and not sure what it actually was that they were supposed to do. Several students asked: "Are we playing tic-tac-toe?" I laughed and then responded, "Maybe." At the time when I started, I couldn't be sure that getting a tic-tac-toe wasn't the goal.

Choice boards are an easy way to promote student choice in learning while also differentiating instruction. To differentiate,

Completa una actividad: DOK

Crea una "nube de palabras" con a menos 25 palabras de tu lista. Usa marcador y también escribe con letras grandes. (wordcloud)	Prepara una conversación con un/a compañero/a, totalmente en español. Memoriza las palabras, a menos de 10 líneas. Flipgrid	Dibuja una escena con a menos de 15 palabras de vocabulario. También escribe un párrafo de 6 frases para describirla en español. Ponla en Padlet también.
Haz un Flipgrid para conversar con amigos, sobre el tema de tu capítulo. Responde a dos personas.	Crea una lección con Nearpod o Formative, con 10 preguntas/actividades interactivas. Serás profesora(a).	Crea un Padlet o Wakelet para hacer preguntas sobre el tema, y también busca imágenes sobre la Red.
Escribe frases con las palabras, a menos 12 frases en español. Edmodo!	Crea un Buncee para enseñar a tus compañeros, más sobre el tema del capítulo.	Un vidéo, un Kahoot, Quizizz, tu opción, pero Pruebalo!!

FIGURE 5.2 An example choice board we have used

we must provide multiple ways for students to process information and build their knowledge. By including a variety of options for practicing with the content, rather than having each student complete the same assignment or worksheet, a choice board offers nine authentic options for students to choose from. We want students to build confidence in learning and encourage them to apply their knowledge in different ways rather than simply repeating or restating the same information. In deciding on the choices to include on the board, I have used the four levels of Norman Webb's Depth of Knowledge as a guide. With Webb's DOK, the four levels are recall, skills and concepts, strategic thinking and extended thinking.

In level one, the recall level, it is basic recall of information, like having students provide a translation or definition, simply remembering information and completing a substitution, perhaps even copying down and defining vocabulary or recognizing words in the target language. Another example might be having students memorize a dialogue in the target language to practice a conversation that helps them build their basic skills and speaking abilities in a more comfortable way.

In level two, these tasks ask students to problem solve, complete steps to determine a solution and maybe classify nouns or verbs. The tasks require students to do more than simply exchange lines of dialogue or translate.

In level three, which is strategic thinking, students explain or perhaps read and draw conclusions about something that they have learned. Students are asked to think perhaps in a more complex or abstract way. This is a good way to have students summarize a reading or to explain something they have learned in their own words without a specific direction other than encouraging them to apply their language skills in new ways. Students might even engage in problem-based learning activities at this level.

In level four, extended thinking requires more complex reasoning or planning. Students might be asked to make connections or compare and contrast, perhaps differences in the language or cultural traditions, for example. Implementing project-based learning where students have to pull information from multiple sources and engage in learning over a longer period of time, requires students to apply their knowledge in a much higher level and would meet the level four of DOK.

It is important for students to feel comfortable with their choices in how to show learning, and using choice boards helps to differentiate instruction and also provides scaffolding for students. The choice board should include options ranging from a more basic level and scaffolded up to a more advanced level, giving students a choice in how to build their skills in a more meaningful and comfortable way. I suggest having the center of the choice board be an activity that all students must complete, whether they start with that space and it is a DOK Level One or maybe it is a DOK Level Four that students build up to completing. One benefit that I didn't foresee when I first tried choice boards was that the products that students end up creating as they work through the choice board become resources that we can then use as teaching tools in our classroom to support students in other classes and in later years.

Choice boards can be done by using paper or created digitally, which means they are great for anywhere learning. You can also choose to make a choice board with 9 squares like I did or include additional squares in four columns with each column focused on a different topic or maybe a different skill (reading, writing, listening, speaking). Whether you set aside one day per week for students to have a choice in an activity to do that day or if it's an enrichment activity for students to choose from, they will enjoy having a lot of different options to explore.

Here Are Some Examples of What My Choice Boards Have Included

Create a game using Kahoot!, Quizizz or Puzz Grid.
Work with a partner to create a game or a word puzzle.
Create a Flipgrid video and invite classmates to respond.
Draw a picture using the vocabulary, label the items and write a description.
Watch a video on YouTube or read an article on Newsela and summarize it.
Design an infographic for illustrating a grammar concept or cultural event.
Write and perform a skit with a classmate.
Create and lead an interactive lesson using Nearpod.
Write a short story or children's book using Buncee.
Record a how-to video using a tool like Screencastify, Educreations or Loom.
Collaborate with a classmate and use Book Creator or StoryJumper.

There are a lot of ideas to choose from that don't require much technology at all. When we give students choices with technology, we help them to build skills beyond the target language.

Explore some simple ideas like having students write an email, record a podcast or create a brochure, which offer more real-world opportunities to practice and apply language skills.

HyperDocs

After trying the "Teacher for a day" and choice boards, I dove into giving HyperDocs a try. Just like choice boards, this was something that I really didn't have any experience with and decided to explore. For anyone unfamiliar with HyperDocs, they are essentially documents with all hyperlinks included that help to promote more interactive and student-directed and student-paced learning activities. HyperDocs involve the use of a Google Doc and follow a specific format. To learn about them, I explored the HyperDocs website (*https://hyperdocs.co/*) and also the book *The HyperDocs Handbook*. Once I created the first few, it was a lot easier to continue to make them for all of my classes. I followed the same structure and simply substituted the activities or content.

Think about the different activities or tools that you use in your classroom and instead of taking the time to set everything up and losing class time due to transitions between activities, place all links and resources into one document through hyperlinks. Students can access the HyperDoc wherever they are. It can be done using stations in the classroom or virtual stations or for students that cannot be in class each day. HyperDocs presented a good option to keep learning going and accessible. Like choice boards, HyperDocs also work well for a hybrid or fully virtual learning environment.

To get started you can check out the HyperDocs website created by the three authors of the HyperDocs Handbook and look at the many examples that are out there for templates. There are even curated lists of HyperDocs created for different grade levels and content areas. As with so many other methods and tools that we bring to our classrooms, there are already starting points that we can use, saving us time and of course encouraging us to take risks with bringing in these new experiences for our students and ourselves.

When I started using them in my classroom, at first students were unsure of what to do. They didn't know how to pace themselves, and having choices like this was something new for them. Be sure to provide some instruction as to how it works and, for some students, be prepared to work with them to set up a plan or timeline for completion. While students may appreciate the choices available for learning, it is helpful to have an action plan to set pacing, at least for the first time using a HyperDoc. Another consideration is using some different tools to create a HyperDoc. I've known some teachers who used Buncee, Padlet or Wakelet

Preterit Tense and Grammar

This is a Hyperdoc. HyperDoc templates are easy to alter, edit, and customize to the structure of the lesson you are creating, just follow the instructions below. Start with **ENGAGE** and **complete each activity** throughout the document. **It is important that you go in order** and **work on your own, taking notes** where indicated. You will need earbuds.

Engage

Please carefully watch the video to **review and learn Irregular** Preterit Tense Uses: (it is in Spanish) https://youtu.be/XGfXA29KUfs **You should take notes, pause video to write down the different verb stems.**

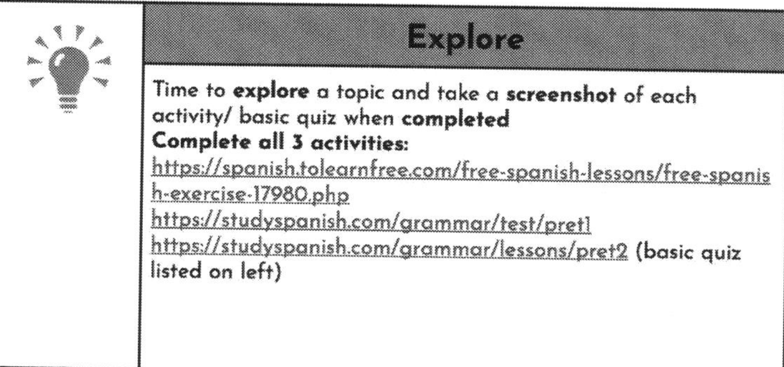

Explore

Time to **explore** a topic and take a **screenshot** of each activity/ basic quiz when **completed**
Complete all 3 activities:
https://spanish.tolearnfree.com/free-spanish-lessons/free-spanish-exercise-17980.php
https://studyspanish.com/grammar/test/pret1
https://studyspanish.com/grammar/lessons/pret2 (basic quiz listed on left)

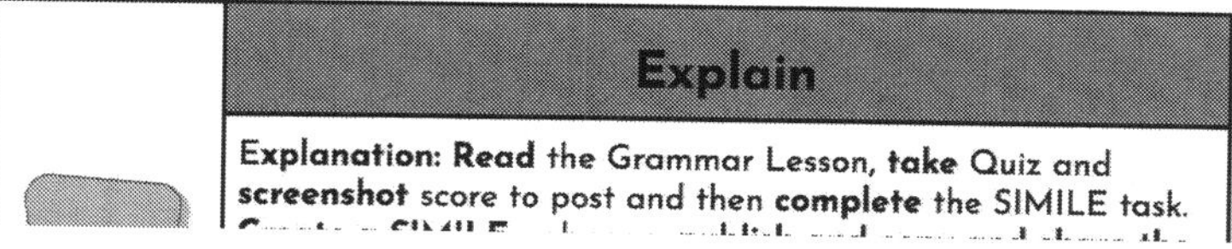

Explain

Explanation: Read the Grammar Lesson, **take** Quiz and **screenshot** score to post and then **complete** the SIMILE task.

FIGURE 5.3 Example of HyperDoc used in Spanish III

and sometimes even Google Slides and created the same type of experience using those virtual spaces.

Next Steps to Place Students in the Lead More

Ever since I made the changes to the look of my classroom and worked to create more opportunities for students who could not be in class each day, I had to continue to come up with new ideas that offered more flexibility and also that enabled students to take more of a lead in their learning. My next step after choice boards and HyperDocs was to explore the concept of genius hour.

A few years ago, when I realized that I hadn't actually been doing authentic project-based learning, I found out about genius hour. Genius hour is a great idea for language classrooms because it is an opportunity for students to explore their passions and interests and then share them with classmates. Because they are deciding what to focus on, they become more comfortable with sharing their "genius" with classmates. Genius hour is inquiry-based and student-driven learning that is infused with student choice and opportunities for authentic language learning experiences. Genius hour, or 20% time, as it has also been referred to, is the time set aside for students to work on their own and come up with ideas for how they will share their knowledge or their project. Some of the many benefits are that it promotes student creativity, sparks curiosity, helps to develop social skills and increases student confidence and comfort in learning. When given the chance to explore something they are curious or passionate about and share it in a collaborative and supportive learning environment, students can build and foster the confidence and comfort needed while learning languages in our classrooms.

When schools closed in March of 2020, I looked for some different ideas to try with my students in my language classes, as meeting together at the same time proved to be a challenge. Another challenge was that not all students had access to our class materials, and so I was looking for some different ideas that would be available for all students. I had done genius hour in my

STEAM course with my 8th graders but not with my language students.

There are many benefits to activities like these as students not only build language skills and acquire more meaningful vocabulary that they will connect with, but they also develop leadership skills. We better understand our students and can build relationships between peers in the classroom and also amplify the learning that happens. When a student can explore a passion or share something they are interested in, it builds more confidence and promotes higher student engagement in learning.

Sharing What You Know

Students are so excited to have time to choose something to learn about. Although at first, for some students, having this freedom to choose what to explore and how to share what they learn can be a bit uncomfortable, after years of choices being made for them, however with the right support, students flourish with this experience. You can feel their excitement, and they are more engaged and invested in learning together. Students will talk about something that matters to them and be able to do so in the target language. Students talk about their genius hour experiences in their other classes and it leads to more teachers trying it in their classrooms as well. Genius hour is another easy way for us to put students in the lead more and for us to be learners right along with them.

My suggestions for getting started are based on how I rolled it out in my classes and my willingness to take the risks. Depending on your grade level and language course, perhaps you choose a theme for the class or have students select their own topic. Either way, students will have to decide upon an independent project. It helps if you can guide students with an essential or driving question or ask them to come up with their own. If choosing a class theme, then perhaps work with students to explore ideas for an essential question. If students are choosing, then ask them for a specific purpose behind why they selected their topic. Students will be able to continue to build their conversational skills and express their opinions, asking for help and relying on already developed language skills for also building new vocabulary related to their topic. We can also create a list of possible ideas for students to explore to give them some direction to head in and also offer a list of guidelines for what they need to come up with as part of their genius hour experience. The main idea is that they explore something of interest and as they learn about it, become more curious and focused on the process of learning and building their language skills and developing cultural awareness.

Next, you want to decide when you will provide time for students in class for working on their genius hour projects. I left the decision up to my students and, like when we did PBL, they decided that Fridays would be the best day. Regardless of whether we are in person, hybrid or virtual, we have a lot of possibilities available through genius hour. In hybrid, perhaps genius hour days will occur on the asynchronous days in our schedule. Creating this time also gives students a break from being online so much, depending on their topics, which is what I found in my own classes during the school closures.

In doing genius hour, we should find ways to promote student conversations and leverage some different spaces in our physical classroom space as well as online so that students can ask questions, share resources, provide feedback and brainstorm if they decide to collaborate with classmates. Previously mentioned tools that would be great for this are things like Padlet, Yo Teach!, Wakelet or a collaborative whiteboard space. See Chapter 3 for more tools for fostering communication.

As with all new methods and tools, it may take a little while to get started with genius hour and find what works, but it just reinforces that learning is a process! Working with students to try something new is a great way to continue to build those connections and add to the classroom culture.

PBL: Empowering Language Learners and Building SEL

As a language teacher, for many years I had assigned projects to my students in all of my courses. I thought for a long time that I was doing PBL with my students. However, after attending some conference presentations and reading some books and blogs, I realized that I had simply been assigning very finite, limited time-span projects to my students. I decided to build my knowledge base and learn about authentic PBL so I could bring it into my classroom.

Over the past few years, PBL has been such a beneficial learning experience for my students as well as a great way for me to learn. Because of all of the information that they shared and their interest in learning more without a focus on grades or a finite project, the impact on our learning was tremendous.

As many of our schools are still potentially either hybrid or fully virtual, it has proven quite beneficial to have strategies or digital tools in our "toolkit" that work well for any transitions we may need to make. PBL is a great option for any grade level or content area and something that can be done in any learning environment.

Throughout our experiences with school closures and uncertainties in the world and education brought on by the pandemic, the positive in it all was that it gave us the push many of us needed to explore new ideas and digital tools, as well as perhaps go back to some prior methods we had used. In my experience, PBL worked well for my students and is a good choice for any content area, grade level, or even teacher experience with using PBL in the classroom. It is also a choice that helps us during any school transitions because we can leverage the different technologies to provide support and feedback for students, for them to share their public product of what they're working on and to create using a variety of possibilities. It's also time for us to think about how we can perhaps have students expand their global awareness and apply their language skills in areas that meet their needs and interests more specifically. To prepare them, we must be prepared to take some risks and explore these methods that bring about powerful student learning opportunities.

As we look for innovative and more student-driven activities that will best prepare them for the future, PBL is a good choice because it is an iterative process that helps students to become more independent and curious learners. We can support students as they shift their focus to the process of learning itself, rather than on a number of points or a final product, and on building their language skills in a way that connects more authentically and meaningfully with their interests. I think that PBL is a great option for all language teachers to explore, especially because the learning space itself does not matter. We can leverage digital tools to give students an opportunity to apply and develop their language skills as they design problems to solve, explore their curiosities and passions and become more socially aware of the world around them. As we prepare them for the future, it is also essential that we help students to shift their focus from the product of learning to the process of learning instead. PBL offers benefits for all classrooms and beyond our content area, and as we look to essential future-ready skills, including the development of SEL skills, we can address the 4 C's: collaboration, communication, creativity and critical thinking. It also empowers students with choice and student-driven learning. We support them as they move from consumers to creators and then to leaders in our classrooms. Once we decide to give PBL a go, we need a digital toolkit for learning anywhere with PBL!

In a hybrid or virtual environment, we can leverage some of the different tools to help students develop social emotional learning skills and provide enrichment opportunities through PBL for our students. These ideas and tools are helpful for creating a sense of belonging, which is important for students.

Amplifying Learning and Connections Through Tech

When we use digital tools to connect our classrooms with other students, educators and experts from around the world, we add to the authenticity and meaningfulness of the learning experiences for all students. Whether we use PBL or challenge/problem-based learning, it leads to more personalized learning through real-world experiences. Something that I often tell my students is that they may not think that they will go on to become a Spanish teacher or that their career will require knowledge of another language however, it's all about having the opportunities and variety in our skill set. I truly believe that giving students the chance to explore careers or an area of interest and uniting that with what they are learning in the target language might help them to identify potential career options for the future, ones which will show the relevance of having language skills.

Through PBL, I have learned more about my students and their personal and future professional aspirations. Over the past couple of years, as I worked to build more cultural and global awareness in the types of activities that I was creating for my students and in the materials that I was bringing in, I started to learn more about the Sustainable Development Goals (SDGs). The SDGs or "global goals" are part of a call to action by the United Nations that are focused on achieving a better and more sustainable future for everyone. The SDGs are focused on 17 goals aimed at eliminating poverty, reducing inequalities, achieving zero hunger, providing quality education and ensuring a sustainable future for all with the target date of 2030. Students who had developed an interest in learning about these very important topics in their other courses connected even more as we worked through PBL in our Spanish classes. This experience led students to become more than simply the consumers in the classroom, but shifted them from creators to the leaders.

For example, some students became interested in careers or community or global initiatives while completing their PBL work. They developed empathy and greater cultural and social

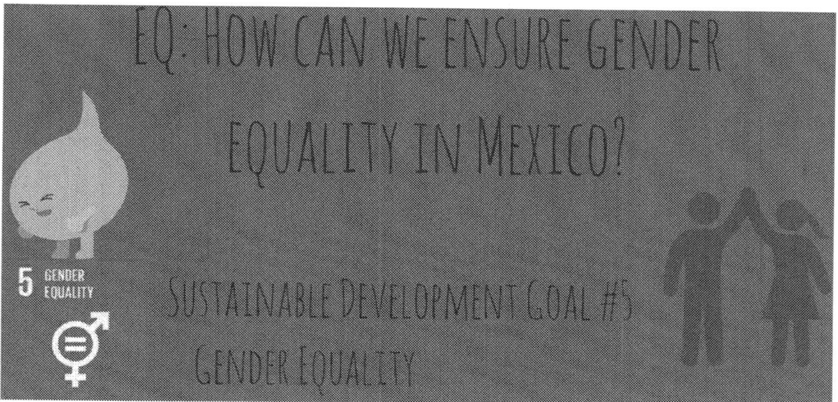

FIGURE 5.4 Buncee PBL presentation focused on SDGs

awareness while building language skills and confidence. Especially important in hybrid or virtual environments, students have to build skills of collaboration and communication and learn to provide feedback to their peers. These are essential skills for the future and it benefits students to have the opportunities to prepare now in our classrooms. To design the most effective and yet choice-filled PBL experiences, there are some common tools that I believe we need to make sure that we have available to our students.

Tools That We Can Use for PBL

1. PBL Platforms. When I first got started with PBL in my Spanish III and IV classes, I leveraged Edmodo as the platform for making those collaborations happen. I connected with a few teachers in Argentina and Spain and used Edmodo as the space for our students to have conversations and collaborate globally. It was a great way to build those relationships and to help students to feel more comfortable asking questions, practicing their writing skills and developing their cultural awareness in the process. There are other possibilities out there, including a platform called Thrively (www.thrively.com). Using Thrively, educators and students can explore a library of standards-aligned projects, which includes rubrics and related documents, videos and website links, which makes it easy to get started. We can make connections with our content and provide a space where students can work with classmates and teachers through the collaboration feed within Thrively. Another option of Thrively, or even using a tool like Edmodo, is that students can build digital portfolios to better track their language learning progress and monitor their goals during the PBL process.
2. Brainstorming and language exchange. Especially in the hybrid or virtual learning spaces, it's important that we have ways for our students to brainstorm together and

build their language skills in more cooperative ways with their peers. We must first make sure that all students have access to devices, so that when we use some of these options, we know that all students have the opportunity to participate in it at their fullest potential. I believe that these types of digital spaces and tools offer many benefits for students to build their confidence and comfort in speaking in front of peers and then with larger groups.

There are so many ways that students can exchange ideas and share resources using whiteboard spaces or other collaborative boards. Some of our favorite options include previously mentioned tools such as Google Jamboard, Padlet, Wakelet, and Whiteboard.chat or relying on the features embedded within Microsoft Teams, Google Classroom or another LMS to create that virtual interactive space. Students can work together and have conversations in the virtual space and feel more closely connected to peers and learning. These options also promote the sharing of student work with a larger public audience, potentially even global collaboration. It is also important for students to have access to not just receive teacher feedback but also to give and receive peer feedback, as these skills are vital for future education and career experiences. We can really expand where students are learning and need to simply start with one idea and try it, see what the student responses are to it and then continue tweaking it until it best fits our particular interests and needs.

3. Power of voice: Something that really was important not just during the school closures as a result of the pandemic but at all times, is the power of voice. The way that we present information for students, the conversations that we have to give feedback or to provide encouragement and also the spaces that we create so students can share their voice with others, matter. Whether in traditional classroom settings or virtual, we need to set up those spaces to provide the support and differentiation that students need as they work through PBL or any learning activity. To best help students grow, we have to be

intentional about setting up a structure or a cycle for providing authentic and timely feedback, which is critical for learning. Students should also have the opportunity to provide peer feedback and communicate and collaborate with classmates. A few tools to explore that offer video and voice features include Anchor, Flipgrid, and Synth. Using Flipgrid, there are thousands of topics available in the library that help to promote inquiry and for students to build language skills by creating and responding to videos. My students have found topics through career explorations on Flipgrid and used these to decide on a PBL focus and then pitched their ideas to classmates. We can also use a tool like VoiceThread (https://voicethread.com/), which encourages students to create and also respond to the discussion in a more interactive way.

4. Reflecting, revising and planning: Just like building language skills, we must help students to reflect on learning, revise and plan next steps in their learning path. It is important that we create spaces for students to work through the phases of PBL, engage in conversations and provide peer feedback in the target language and build global awareness. We can gather responses by using tools like Google or Microsoft Forms or choose a video response tool like Flipgrid or Synth, perhaps, or create digital whiteboard spaces for more collaboration. These options promote the development of communicative and interpersonal skills and also develop SEL skills at the same time. In the past, I also used Kidblog and Spaces EDU with my students because it created a space to build writing skills and help students to become more comfortable in sharing their learning and developing language skills. These options would also be highly beneficial for students completing them by responding in the target language. We can amplify learning opportunities for students using PBL with digital tools, to develop language skills, build vital SEL skills, and engage in more authentic and personalized learning experiences which do not depend on a specific learning environment.

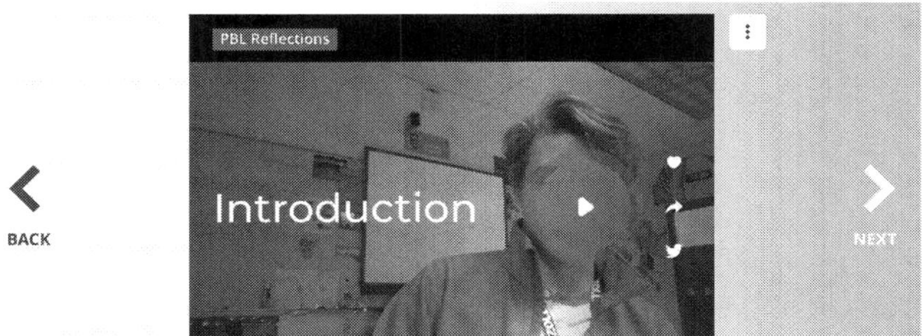

FIGURE 5.5 Student response to PBL reflection on Synth

As we consider these focus areas for PBL and how to infuse PBL with language learning, we can see how powerful these opportunities can be for students. When we continue to bring in more ways for students to not only learn together, but to lead each other through their learning journeys and build relationships while developing their language skills in a supportive space, students will thrive.

For PBL or genius hour as mentioned earlier, these are some options for tools to facilitate the PBL process and also that can be used for daily assessments, check-ins and lesson creation for and by students. Some of the options are available for free to educators and some have multiple subscription types. There are enough choices using the free accounts for each of these choices. During hybrid and virtual learning, each of these enabled me to really stay connected with students, to facilitate conversations and check-in on progress as well as create more interactive lessons for my students.

Teaching a language virtually, it can be a challenge to find the best tools to foster the development of speaking, reading, writing and listening skills, however the tools and ideas that follow will, in some cases, create the right space for us to provide practice and support for students in each of these areas. Here are five areas that we need to focus on regardless of where learning is happening and some tools to consider.

1. Better Global Collaboration. We need options to encourage students to collaborate both in and out of our

classrooms and with PBL, to share their work with global peers. With digital spaces like Padlet (www.padlet.com) or Wakelet (www.wakelet.com), which is free, students can interact, share resources and include different media formats. With Wakelet, students can record a Flipgrid video, and it also offers the Immersive Reader, which can help to build confidence in speaking in the target language and for communicating with students from around the world. We can amplify the options by using tools like either Whiteboard.chat (www.whiteboard.chat) or Whiteboard.fi, which are free whiteboard spaces with versatile tools and functions for our classes. Students can have their own whiteboard to share their work with the teacher or classmates and these spaces promote collaboration regardless of the learning space. An additional benefit is that students continue to build digital citizenship skills while working in these virtual spaces together.

2. Check-ins and SEL. It is always important to have a way to check in with our students, to see how they're doing with the content, to better understand any areas that they might be struggling with and also to do a quick assessment. There's no shortage of options to use; it comes down to the type of information that we want. Do we want some quick questions that may be all choice or open-ended responses or do we want to actually hear from students and prefer to use something that offers the ability to record audio or video? Fun activities might be to create an image with nine different pictures and ask students to post which image most closely relates to how they're feeling, or we can use tools like Flipgrid, Quizizz, or SurveyMonkey (www.surveymonkey.com) to create an audio response or survey. I also enjoy sending quick Buncee messages in our Microsoft Teams meetings.
3. Engaging peers in lessons. With so many schools in hybrid or fully virtual learning, we need more ways to engage students in learning, by providing more interactive lessons and PBL presentations through options like GoFormative, (www.goformative.com), Nearpod (www.

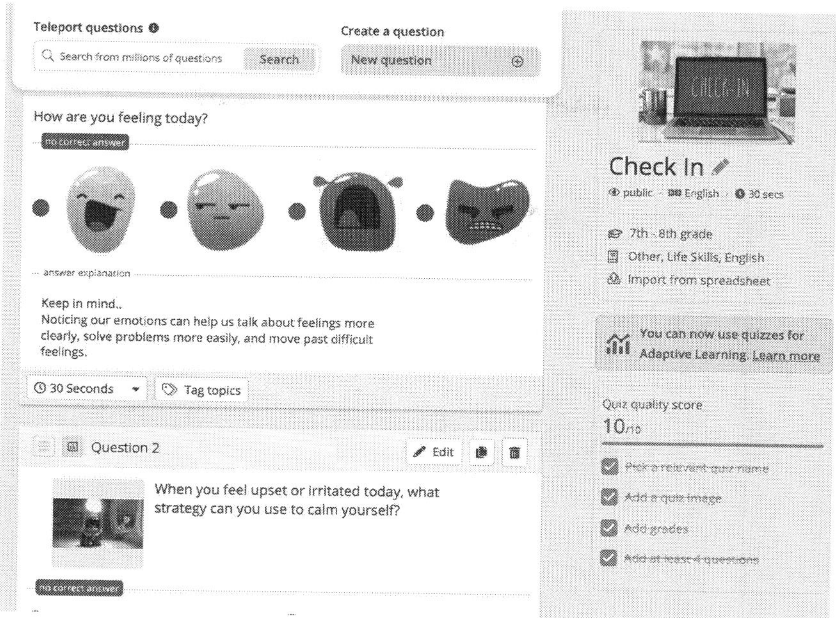

FIGURE 5.6 Quizizz game used for a check-in for any course

nearpod.com), or Pear Deck (www.peardeck.com). As a teacher, we can use these tools to teach students about PBL and create spaces for students to share what they are learning and explore more closely. Depending on the age of our students (my students are in grades 9 through 12), we can have students create their own lessons to share their learning with classmates. What a game changer for students to design a Nearpod lesson with classmates to share with students in Argentina and Spain!

4. Spark curiosity for language learning! Whether through PBL and student choices in learning or the global connections we make, students become more excited for learning and practicing a language. While it can make students nervous to speak in the target language, by providing more personalized choices and using tools that promote discussion, such as *Flipgrid* or *Synth*, we provide students with a comfortable space to share what they are

FIGURE 5.7 Student created Nearpod lesson for PBL

learning. These are also wonderful spaces for educators to provide direct, authentic feedback to each student while continuing to foster vital relationships and a love of language learning throughout the year.

5. Writing and reflective practice: Students need opportunities to write, and if we want non-digital options, we can use paper or sticky notes as a way to have students share reflections on not only their own work but also on the work of their peers. Blogging and daily journaling are options that I have used in my classes and my own daily practice. For language learners, encouraging students to write down their thoughts as they are working on their PBL, will provide them with something tangible to go back to as they plan new goals and evaluate their own work. It creates a way for students to self-assess and develop their awareness of their language growth. Depending on the grade level, we also have digital options that promote more collaboration between students and teachers. Using options such as Kidblog (Fan School), Edublogs (www.edublogs.org), or creating a space using Microsoft Teams

or Google Classroom helps teachers and students to build writing skills and set new goals for their language development. Other tools like Gimkit Ink can be a great space for students to build writing skills. We also have to help students to build the essential skills for not only the future, but that they need now as we are finding ourselves using more technology for our learning experiences.

6. Brainstorming ideas for developing language skills: It is important that we push students to apply language skills at a higher level. We can do this by asking students to name the top five or ten challenges in an area of the world where the target language is spoken. Students could make their choice based on geography, a certain industry of interest or perhaps students can be tasked to come up with a list of things they notice about their community or in the world around them. When we provide these types of opportunities, we push students to think differently about language learning. They make a connection with something that is a personal interest or that they are curious about and that will give them the more authentic and meaningful connection to practice those skills with real-world applicability.

Give students space to develop plans for how to solve these challenges or how they could have solved them better. When my students have done this in our classroom, they worked together to solve a problem they found in a Spanish-speaking country. They did a lot of research and invested in learning about the issue they focused on, but also learning new and relevant vocabulary. They chose to create a presentation or a collaborative book, which became resources we could refer to later in the year or for other students to use as a way to build their language skills too.

In the educator examples which follow, you can see some different activities and how to use them to help students to build their confidence and leadership skills in the classroom. When students can work together with peers on a collaborative effort, it helps them to become more comfortable and that comfort transfers into their willingness to engage in learning activities and speaking up more in the classroom.

Karina del Castillo, Spain

Implementing online tools like Book Creator (www.bookcreator.com) and Google Slides was a highlight in my first school year online. Adding the final versions of the book to our virtual libraries was a great way to share the hard work from my students. We did four libraries during the whole school year, and I was able to see the growth from the first books and the last one.

https://docs.google.com/presentation/d/1uoTuk6XmRN1AyqQ9O1dm3290gygfZ3y06X9XXm2AoIl/edit?usp=sharing

Katie Bordner, Pittsburgh, PA

Creating a Yearbook

- One of the ways I recycle vocabulary topics is to discuss preferences in the class. When talking about school, we talk about different types of teachers (super-smart, super-fun, super-wise, etc.). When we talk about food, we discuss our favorite restaurants and meals. For activities, we talk about things we like/don't like to do. When talking about the calendar, we discuss our favorite holidays/seasons.
- This is also an easy-to-recycle method if you teach multiple grades/levels because you can "level up" the difficulty of the conversation while still using the same vocabulary. At the lower level you're using "I like," "I don't like," "I love" and "I hate." At more advanced levels you're asking *why* they like/love/hate the particular preference.
- I will survey the students and summarize what the preferences are in the target language through the method "Write and Discuss" (Chase, 2019). I've been using Canva (*www.canva.com*) to type up my summaries because I love how you can insert images/icons to aid in comprehension. For example, I will insert an image of a book above the word *libro*. (Eventually when we are back together, it could be a student's job to type up with summary or insert images.) The key here is that the summary is short, just a paragraph or so. I will then reuse these texts in future classes for warm-ups to review previously taught content, to show examples of grammatical structures, or for listening comprehension assessments. I might add more details for a reading comprehension assessment as well. When I use these for assessments, I pick a summary from another class so I'm assessing comprehension and not how well they remember the conversation.
- I will also print the summaries and bind them together. This becomes a book option for FVR (Free Voluntary Reading), which is a great option for lower-level readers because it is familiar with lots of images to make it comprehensible. An added bonus is that when students see the published work, they are more likely to participate in the discussions because they want to be written about!
- Chase, A. (2019, January 3). *Write & Discuss: How do I love thee? Let me count the ways*. Loading up my little darlings with Comprehensible Input. Retrieved January 13, 2021, from *https://senorachase.com/2019/01/03/write-discuss/*

Kristen Lyon

Every year my students study the artwork of Fernando Botero. We learn relevant vocabulary and about the artist and his style. At the end of the unit, students can take the role of artist, journalist, museum guide, critic, etc. to share their knowledge. Some students will paint their own versions of a Botero painting, describe one of their favorites using Flipgrid and/or screen record, or create an interview with the artist.

Laura Steinbrink

Reaching the deeper levels of rigor and getting students to think critically while learning a world language can seem difficult. A lot of what students have to learn initially is that surface-level knowledge, but using pictures without words is one way you can get students swimming in the deep end of the thinking pool. You might now be thinking that I am about to drop some serious work on you, but this activity does not require much from you other than finding or creating a picture that suits your learning objectives. The trick to moving the learning from surface to deep is the number of decisions students have to make and providing problems that have multiple correct answers or more than one possible product.

Activity:

Learning target: Students can use the correct conjugated verb form of regular -ER verbs in a sentence.

For that learning target, you need a picture that allows students to infer the verb needed, provides something to extend the sentence, and has multiple decisions that need to be made about the subject to use in the sentence. You can use this one day as an oral activity and a different day as a written activity. I like to have several slides of images so that students can practice multiple times. Every student has to come up with a unique sentence out loud based on the same picture.

Instructions: Based on the picture say a sentence in the target language that can be inferred from what you see:

In the first picture, students need to figure out what verb will be in play. The platter of cheese indicates that they need to use the verb *comer*. The mixed gender of the subjects means students have to make decisions about what pronoun to use if they decide to go that route for the subject. Students can continue creating sentences by varying the subject. Students can be asked to write or say as many sentences as they can from the pictures you present either digitally or in person.

There are many possible answers, so students are required to analyze the pictures, make decisions about the subject, verb, and rest of the information to include in the sentence. Students have to make sure that their sentence is unique when it is their turn. This activity can be used in all sorts of ways once your students master the concept of the activity.

FIGURE 5.8 Buncee-created images to use for writing and speaking prompts

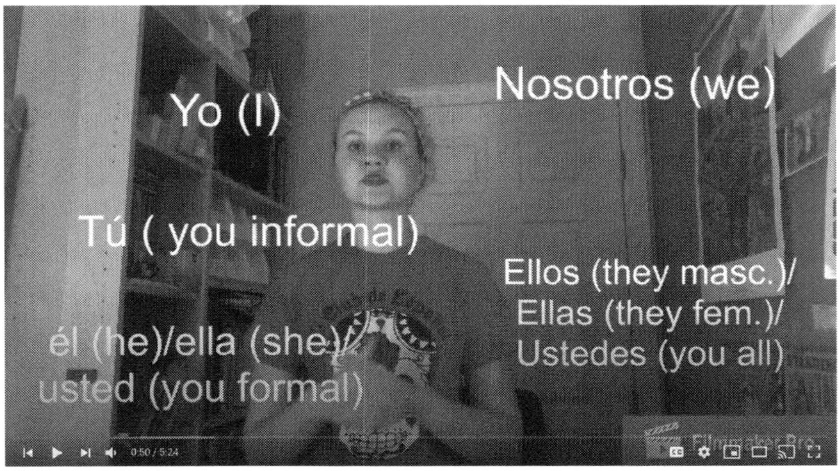

FIGURE 5.9 Student-created video lesson for Spanish I students on verb conjugations

Laura's activity is a good opportunity to help students to build their confidence and also to take more of a lead in classroom discussions and activities. I have always enjoyed seeing what students come up with, especially as they progress through each year of Spanish and become excited to share their knowledge with others, take a lead in the classroom and also help other students who are building their language skills. One of my favorite examples of this was a student who created some tutorial videos on verb conjugations for students in Spanish I. It was not something that she was asked to do, she simply decided to create one because she loved Spanish and loved creating and editing videos!

It is all about the opportunities that we create and the support that we provide for our students along their journey. There are so many benefits for educators when we create opportunities for students to take the lead in the classroom. It helps us to move into more of a facilitator and co-learner role with our students because of all of the new knowledge that they can bring in as they explore topics of interest, build vocabulary in new ways, and become more engaged in and excited for learning a language.

6

Strategies and Tools That We Can Use to Help Students Create Global Connections

Chapter Summary

In this chapter, you will learn many ideas for having students show and share what they know. Whether they design their own assessments using some of the multimedia options or create a presentation to share with classmates or a larger audience, the goal is to empower students to collaborate more and make global connections. The focus is on providing a more authentic and meaningful way to show learning, through options such as interactive lessons, videos and other presentation formats. The methods and tools will be applicable to in-person and remote learning and provide a variety of quick ideas to get started in your classroom to help students develop their language skills and build confidence to take the lead more.

What to expect in this chapter:

- Ways to create a global learning community
- Ideas for building confidence in learners
- Explore tools and methods that promote essential future-ready skills

DOI: 10.4324/9781003137665-7

It has been an interesting time in education since school closures in March of 2020. We experienced transitions from fully remote, to hybrid, to in-person instruction and sometimes with very little notice, if any at all. Sometimes we transitioned multiple times in a week, requiring us to always be prepared to keep learning going and remain flexible in our practice. Something that I learned even more from that experience was the importance of being connected and the impact on our students from being able to collaborate with other students from around the world. Something that has helped to keep consistency in learning and connecting was leveraging the right digital tools and spaces to keep learning going and to create ways for students and teachers to collaborate, regardless of the type of learning environment we might find ourselves in. Through these experiences, we were challenged to try new ideas, to find new ways to learn and to continue to reflect on our journey as we planned for the future.

Before the pandemic and push to trying new ideas and facilitating collaboration with our students and their families, I spent time exploring ways to connect my students with students from Spanish-speaking countries. A few times I had set up for my students to have a pen pal, but most of the time those connections didn't work out because mail was lost or due to another disconnect in the communication. It became an area that I wanted to work on in my classroom. To expand on what my students were learning, as mentioned earlier, I started to do PBL (project-based learning) with my students. Initially, we focused on simply learning about PBL and sharing the work with students in our own classroom. However, entering our second year of doing PBL, we took it to another level with my Spanish classes.

In 2017, I had an opportunity to present at EdmodoCon, an online and in-person event held by Edmodo, an LMS, that connected me with educators from around the world. Before the event, I was amazed at the power of technology to unite the group of speakers using WhatsApp. During the event, there were many opportunities to get to know one another and explore ideas for using Edmodo in our classrooms. My experience inspired me to do more in my classroom to foster global connections.

it so difficult to get other teachers to participate in this wonderful idea.
I believe that next year we could do much better! The school year finishes in November, here in Argentina, so we are getting to the final exams.
Personally, I am thrilled working with you and I hope we can continue so. I'm eager to learn about all of you and I'm really interested and I've started digging into PBL, which I've never actually tried.
Hope we can contact soon.

FIGURE 6.1 Beginning conversation on Edmodo to start our PBL collaboration with teacher in Argentina

Being able to learn from such diverse perspectives and background experiences, plus the ability to communicate instantly with my new colleagues from eight different countries, further solidified my belief that I must create similar opportunities for my students to connect and learn from others. Students need to have as many diverse, authentic opportunities to explore the world and learn from others as they can. Prior to EdmodoCon, I was not sure where to begin. It does take time to decide on the best method and structure to use, but I took a chance and found it to be really quite simple through Edmodo.

The first year of doing PBL, students learned about one another as they worked together and were focused on the learning experience. They explored Spanish-speaking countries and topics that were important in those places or that were important to them. We can focus on building skills in the target language while helping students to develop a greater awareness of the language community and make comparisons between the different cultures and language being studied. To take the next step, I looked to Edmodo to make connections with other classrooms and found two teachers interested in working with us. While I used Edmodo, there are also professional learning communities available through ISTE (International Society for Technology in

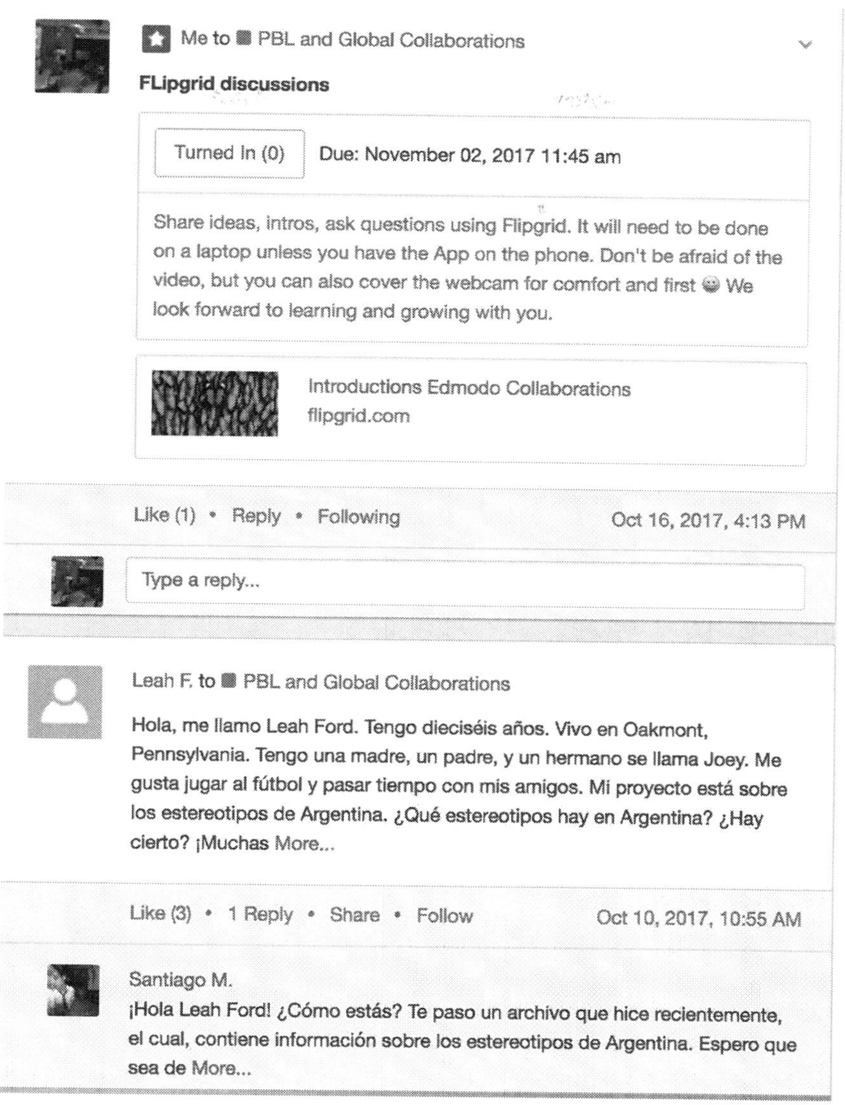

FIGURE 6.2 Space created on Edmodo for students to connect and learn about one another

Education), Flipgrid and even communities on Facebook for language educators. Getting started simply takes posting a message in one of these and waiting for responses from educators who are equally as interested in making new connections.

Thinking back to how we started, I only wish that I would have given it a try sooner. However, I didn't realize how much more quickly it can be facilitated through the digital tools available to us today. When I look at the changes we have seen in the areas of education and work since March of 2020, the amount of technology that we use has continued to increase as we find new ways to connect and facilitate the "new normal." We had to learn and teach in isolation for extended periods of time, which is not easy, especially when learning needs to be social and we need opportunities to regularly communicate and collaborate with each other. I have long believed in the power of sharing our stories and especially when it comes to our language classrooms. It is essential that students learn as much as they can about the culture and the people who speak the language that they are studying. Learning spaces and strategies are changing, and we now have options for students to more actively learn and explore the world from within our classrooms or in the virtual space.

Sharing Our Work

When it comes to PBL, one of the elements requires that students' work be publicly displayed, discussed and critiqued. We know that presenting to one's classmates can be scary, but we need to create opportunities for our students to share their work not just in our classrooms, but beyond our classroom walls and school community. As you have read, during our PBL we used multiple tools to facilitate the exchange of information with the students in Argentina and Spain. Students first shared their work on a global scale by using a Padlet, where all students posted photos, asked questions and shared resources. Students developed their skills of collaboration years ago through our PBL experience, and this helped them to be better prepared when schools closed and we worked through the changing learning environments. Technology enabled students to connect to their global peers and ask questions about school, family traditions, and important issues facing students today. Through experiences such as these, they not only learned about one another, but they had a more interactive way to more deeply understand different cultures and experiences.

Building Social Awareness Through Global Sharing

At the beginning and throughout the school year, we need to get to know our students and continue to build those relationships so that we can provide the best support for them in our classrooms. With a greater focus on social-emotional learning (SEL), we need to provide opportunities for students to develop their self-awareness, while also developing social awareness as they work together with classmates and global peers. Especially now, with so many changes in the way school looks and what experiences students are having, we must be intentional about providing the right methods and tools for students to develop SEL skills and learn to navigate in the physical and digital space.

The beginning of the year is always a great time to try some of the new ideas that we learned about over the summer and improve on methods used in the past school year. It's also a very important time for continuing to build those relationships that are so fundamental to the learning that happens in our classrooms. One way that I really enjoy getting to know my students is by the different types of work and projects that I offer them in my classes. For many years, I was assigning projects with specifics about what students had to create and left little room for their own choice in creating. However, after some students started to change the project requirements on their own, I realized that I needed to change my teaching practice to allow for more of that. I've really seen a big difference in my classroom when it comes to student learning and confidence.

When students have a chance to create evidence of what they are learning and infuse who they are, sharing their interests and experiences with us and their audience, it totally amplifies their learning potential. Our students need to have options that encourage and empower them to express what they're learning in a way that is unique and meaningful to them. As educators, we will have to be creative and ready to take some risks with trying some of the different tools out there. We can select a few of the most versatile ones to add to our toolkit, which is always a good place to start.

Telling Our Stories Globally

One of the best ways that I've been able to learn more about my students and that has helped them connect with the content in a more authentic way is through digital storytelling. By giving students more choices in what to create, whether they want to draw, take pictures, make a slideshow, create a video or come up with their own innovative idea, we will empower students with more authentic and personalized learning opportunities. It's all about choices and offering enough so that each student finds something to meet their needs and personal interests and that enables them to grow and reflect in the process. It's also important to help students develop essential skills, like SEL and digital citizenship skills, which are vital for them now and in the future. For students, digital storytelling helps them to share who they are and what they are learning with their own unique viewpoint and perspective. Through these experiences, they can better connect with classmates and go beyond the classroom space and share with students and educators from around the world.

We have powerful digital tools available that enable us to not only create and share but also to collaborate with students from other classrooms. Talk about leveraging the power of technology to help students to develop those vital SEL skills and to become socially aware and be more invested in learning because they are learning and creating with purpose.

With digital storytelling, students can collaborate on a digital book or leverage some of the audio and video tools available to share what they are learning and create together.

I have noticed that students are more excited about creating with the language when they have options that promote creativity, spark their curiosity and engage them in a new way to apply their language skills.

Knowing where to begin can take time to sort through the options however, here are a few to start with in your classroom. Each of these tools provide choices for students regardless of where learning is actually taking place. Using one or all of these options throughout the year will help with any transitions we need to make and will keep educators learning right along with and from students.

1. Animoto (www.animoto.com). I first used Animoto to create a quick video to introduce digital storytelling to students in my STEAM course. Students first made videos to introduce themselves at the start of the year and also to retell a story that they had read in their English class. For language teachers, Animoto can be used as a way to get to know our students, especially if we are not starting the year in-person and want to learn about their interests. Using Animoto does not require a lot of time to get started and therefore students can focus on creating with the language and having fun in the process. For students who might be hesitant to speak in class, choosing Animoto enables them to do their introductions by creating a short video about themselves and build comfort in the classroom.

We can use Animoto to have students create video newsletters, book reports or summaries, a travel story or they can choose from the other templates to create something that interests them. Educators can also use Animoto to teach a lesson about new vocabulary or verbs or for creating a welcome message for

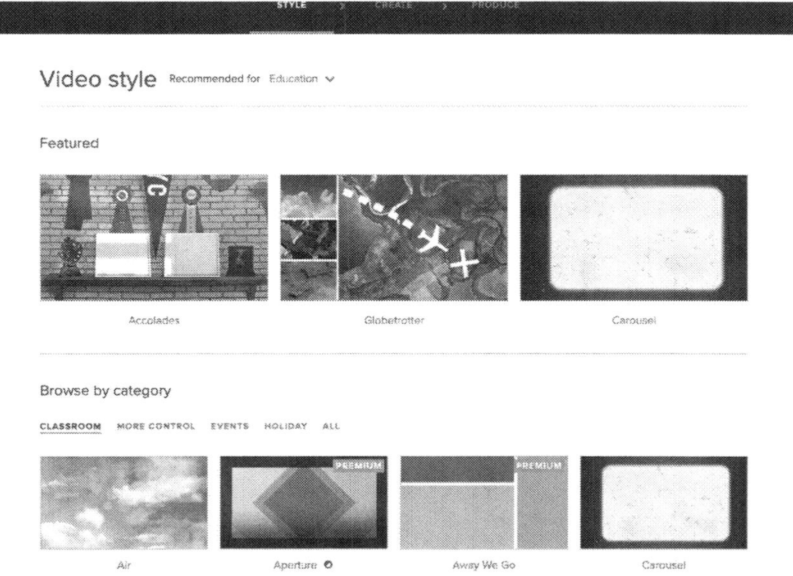

FIGURE 6.3 Animoto videos and theme options

students. Educators can apply for a free classroom *account* with Animoto.

(*https://animoto.com/business/education*).

2. Buncee. Mentioned several times throughout the book, Buncee offers a lot when it comes to learning. It has been my favorite for years and is always the tool that students are excited to create with in my classes. For a few ideas, we can use Buncee to teach a lesson or create a check-in with our students or have students share their genius hour or PBL through a Buncee! A powerful way to use Buncee is for digital storytelling and sharing stories with students globally. We can connect in different educator communities, whether on Facebook or Twitter, and have our students create an "About Me" Buncee or share ideas, interests, experiences by creating a Buncee from scratch. With the features of the platform, students can record audio and video, which makes it even more authentic and personal. Buncees can be shared on a collaborative Buncee Board and enjoyed by everyone without worry about language barriers as it has Immersive Reader, so students can find the language they need or are interested in and be able to read the story or learn about one another in this space. A few years ago, students created Buncees to share with children who were spending the holidays in the hospital. More than 1,000 Buncees with stories, audio and video were added to a collaborative board where people from around the world could explore and learn different cultures and experiences. Students working together on a common goal or for a kindness act or purpose will benefit in many ways beyond the language and cultural awareness they are obtaining from it.
3. Elementari. For language educators looking to bring in some STEM/STEAM-focused activities into the classroom, Elementari is a great choice. It is a platform for students in grades K through 12 that provides a space for creating and remixing interactive stories. Elementari uses visual coding and works well whether for in-person

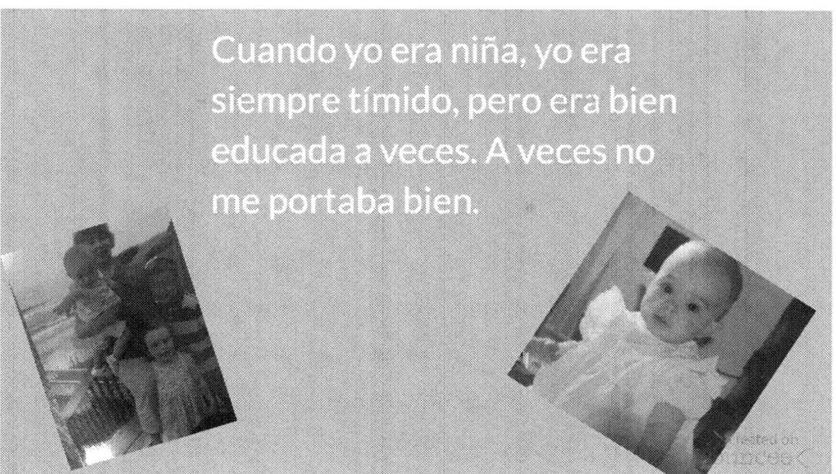

FIGURE 6.4 Buncee project completed by a Spanish II student about their childhood

or remote learning. Students can create engaging stories by choosing from the professional illustrations, background sounds and effects and animations to design their own. Elementari is a great option for bringing coding and STEM into the language classroom and teachers can explore the *curriculum* to find lessons to get started with. Elementari integrates with Google Classroom and does not require any downloads or installations of software.

4. Genially. Genially is a versatile and interactive platform to create interactive images, presentations and even digital escape rooms. There are so many options for what can be added into your presentation like sound, hyperlinks, social media buttons and so much more. The best thing about it is that there are so many ready-made templates and options to choose from that it is easy and quick to get started. Genially is collaborative, so you can work with other educators or have students work together on the same project. As we may need to work through transitioning learning environments, having a space for students to collaborate and create makes a difference. Students in my Spanish II class created a travel ad to a Spanish speaking country and wrote a postcard as though

FIGURE 6.5 Project with Genially, writing a children's book

they took the trip. Students in Spanish III created news reports and infographics for what to do in an emergency.

5. Storybird. (www.storybird.com) We have used Storybird in my classes for years, and what I love the most about it is that it offers so many choices for students to write a story and bring it to life. I first used it when I was getting my master's degree and had to create a book about key laws and rulings in special education. I really enjoyed creating with it and based on my own experience, decided that I needed to provide a similar opportunity for my students. I thought that they would enjoy creating and that perhaps it would encourage them to be more descriptive in their writing based on the scenes and artwork they chose for their story. All of the artwork is provided within the Storybird platform, and so students simply need to decide on a theme and then add in their text to make their book.

Students have the option to download or print their story as a soft or hardcover book. For many years, students in my Spanish classes have used Storybird to create their own books, many of which we have then printed for use in our classroom. There are

FIGURE 6.6 Printed copy of a Storybird book

thousands of options for backgrounds and themes to choose from as well as books to explore and read.

6. Storyboard That (www.storyboardthat.com) has been a favorite of many of my students over the years. It is a tool that I first learned about from one of my seventh graders in Spanish I. Storyboard That is an online tool for students or anyone to tell a story in a comic strip presentation style. We have used it in all levels of Spanish as well as my STEAM course and students enjoy choosing from different backgrounds, characters, props, scenes, speech bubbles and so much more. It is easy to get started with and students can really personalize the characters, which creates a very authentic and meaningful representation of the story they are trying to tell or the concepts they are trying to visualize.

Another benefit of Storyboard That is that with a teacher account, you can see student projects and choose from world language lesson plans and examples available for French and Spanish, which make it easier to get started right away. You can customize the templates available to create your own lesson. For teaching other world languages, simply choose from the templates available and adjust to meet your specific content and language level needs. Some added features are that students can present their project in class or download as a GIF, PDF or PowerPoint. All text is included below the presentation with all image attributions provided.

7. StoryJumper (www.storyjumper.com). It is easy to get started with StoryJumper and students will enjoy creating characters and choosing the appearance, clothing and more to truly personalize their story. I spent some time on my own learning about all of the features of StoryJumper and then included it as one of the options for Spanish III students to write their own book. Two students decided to use it for their midterm project and added me as a collaborator so that I could work with them as they revised their work and needed some help with accent marks. It is a tool that can be used for learning at school or home and makes it fun for students to create, collaborate, illustrate, and narrate in the target language. There are writing lesson plans and story starter ideas available to explore (www.storyjumper.com/class/lessons#me). For language educators, it is fun to explore the books available online. Similar to some of the other options, you can create books for your students and download or print books that students create. StoryJumper offers materials in several languages, including French, Greek, Italian,

FIGURE 6.7 StoryJumper children's book written by Spanish III

Lithuanian, Spanish and Turkish as well as different categories available, including Roblox and Minecraft.

8. Zigazoo (www.zigazoo.com). My Spanish II students enjoyed trying Zigazoo out for the first time in the spring of 2020. I decided to explore some new tools, and Zigazoo was first on my list. It is a free video sharing app where students can create a short video in response to daily prompts and has a similar look and experience to Instagram and TikTok, which is why my students liked using it. For their first prompt, they described their favorite clothing and what they would wear for certain events or special occasions. Students responded that they enjoyed using Zigazoo more than some of the other video response tools that we had used.

It is easy to create an account with Zigazoo and have students join in to share their responses. You can create your own prompt or explore the different educator channels and assign a prompt to a class. My friend Laura Steinbrink, an educator from Missouri who also teaches Spanish, has her own Spanish channel. She creates a prompt for younger students to learn Spanish and share their learning with others. Each video can be up to a length of 30 seconds. Each day there are featured projects and the Zigazoo app gives students a fun way to think about and try new things. It is also a great option for project-based learning types of activities and asking students to respond to peers or provide an idea for a prompt. It creates an opportunity to spark curiosity for learning and increase student engagement.

Each of the options above provide students with different choices in how to show what they are learning. What is even better is that several of them even offer possibilities for collaboration, which is great for students, especially when working in virtual learning environments or preparing for possible transitions throughout the school year. We just need to know enough to get them started and then let them take it in their own direction. Doing this makes all the difference and, from what I've seen in my own classroom, also leads to an increase in student engagement and a true excitement for learning. We can even use Google

Slides and have students collaborate with students not just in their classroom but from classrooms around the world. Of course, it requires that we focus on digital citizenship and respect one another's work that we're adding into that collaborative space, but the benefits are far-reaching. With these tools we can share who we are and learn more about the experiences of others while fostering the acquisition of skills in the target language.

Expressing and Sharing Ideas Through Conversations

Beyond the options for writing a book or creating a collaborative presentation, there are many other activities and tools that can help students share who they are, although not all students will feel comfortable with each option we provide. Whether we ask them to speak in front of the classroom, answer questions during class, or engage in activities like icebreakers or other team-building activities, some students may be quite hesitant or become nervous about engaging in these types of activities. We need to help students build their comfort with public speaking and become confident in communicating with others. It is important to get to know one another and build relationships, whether we are in our physical classrooms or working together in digital spaces, so we must have a few different options and formats available to us and our students. A question to consider is: What can we do to help reduce and ideally eliminate the fears that hold our students back from sharing who they are and telling their stories with us and others? How can we promote the development of our social presence?

There are many options available to create our social presence by leveraging tools in the virtual space. Something that I referred to in Chapter 1 about my own experience with online learning and that students noted at the end of the 2019–20 school year and well throughout the 2020–21 school year, is just how important it is to feel connected to others in the classroom and in life. We need something in place that will help to foster those connections throughout the year, especially as we transition between school and distance learning spaces, if needed.

Here are four additional ideas to help students express themselves and connect globally in the digital age.

1. Blog and creative writing. As we help our students to develop their language skills, we have to find ways to split time so that we are providing opportunities for them to build their listening, reading, speaking and writing skills. A practice that helps with the development of multiple skills at the same time is blogging. We can choose from digital tools or rely on paper and pen to have our students blog. It is beneficial for building their language skills in multiple ways and also for tracking their personal growth over time as a digital portfolio of their work. It's also a way for them to connect with others beyond their own classroom community. We can bring in some really wonderful and enriching learning experiences for our students to write and share with a public audience. We have to remember to be mindful of the privacy of our students when we set up any collaborations with another classroom.

Whether using a traditional notebook or a blogging tool like Kidblog or Edublogs, or by creating a space within an LMS or other learning platform, blogging is such a helpful way for students to express themselves and build comfort and confidence in learning. It provides students with a digital space to build their online presence and be able to exchange ideas with their teacher and peers. In addition to blogging tools, using an option like Book Creator (*www.bookcreator.com*) can

Ide Koulbanis

My class enjoyed participating in the Global Write with Bronwyn Joyce, an educator from Australia. My World Cultures classes created Buncees to respond to her weekly prompts.

We also planned an additional collaboration where my students in Rhode Island and her students in Australia would respond to a documentary we were all watching called "On The Way To School." I was super excited to foster these global connections with others.

We also regularly take part in initiatives such as the Global Buncee Book, International Dot Day, DigCit Summit and Digital Learning Day . . . all great ways to help my students become global learners with others across the globe.

provide a collaborative space for students to introduce themselves and tell their story in what becomes a class book!

2. Videos and vlogging. Especially when we are working with hybrid or fully virtual learning environments, it's important to build relationships and have opportunities to interact with our classmates and teachers. There are a lot of possibilities for using video for creating in a language classroom. A simple way to start is to have students use their phone camera or other device to record a short self-introduction and share with classmates or just their teacher. For students who may be hesitant to appear on camera, there are some fun tools to try like Snapchat (students 13 and older) or Tellagami or Voki. Students can create an avatar to portray themselves and then record their message. We can use Flipgrid, which enables students to add in a background and use some of the special effects to dress up or to add in some fun stickers to their presentation. For global collaborations, whether through PBL activities or setting up pen pals for our students, we can use these videos to share with other classrooms and learn about one another. Finding a GridPal (pen pal through Flipgrid) is another easy way to get started with building some global learning communities for you and your students. As Jimena shares below, using Postcrossing for pen pals is also a good option for students who wish to receive real postcards in the mail from around the world. A great way to practice their language skills!
3. A photo story. Using tools like Animoto (www.animoto.com) or Adobe Spark (www.spark.adobe.com) students can quickly share photos or find

> **Luis Oliveira**
>
> Microsoft Teams is used as our learning environment. In addition to being a great place to work, it is also a tremendous communication tool. We use Teams throughout the year to meet and connect with other groups around the world. When the Skype in the Classroom activities moved to Flipgrid, the Flipgrid sessions will embed within Teams as well.

> **Jimena Licitra**
>
> Students can create global connections using GridPals from Flipgrid or Postcrossing (www.postcrossing.com/) Postcrossing is a wonderful place to connect with other learners and practice writing in real life.
>
> As for Flipgrid, I have used it in many ways. My favorite exchange was with a Chicago school. We created a new topic every month and kids posted videos about that topic. They were learning Spanish and my students were English learners. It was an awesome experience because my students made videos in English and Spanish and realized how difficult it was for them to understand the Spanish accents. We discovered American traditions for Halloween, Christmas and we got to know about their school. I remember one specific activity which involved rubrics on Flipgrid. The American teacher gave an assignment to their students where they had to represent a daily life situation (going shopping, cooking, doing laundry. . .). She created a rubric on Flipgrid and my students and I sent our feedback with that rubric and added personal comments. Everybody loved the experience!!! All students participated and agreed that this was the most enriching experience they had had.

images that represent who they are and quickly create a short video to share with classmates and for global collaborations. With these two options, students can choose to create with only text or add audio to create a short video clip. Using Animoto and Adobe Spark were good choices for my Spanish I and II students, who were working on family projects and wanted to create something that they could share with family and friends. What a meaningful and purposeful learning experience to be shared with families! Especially at the start of the year, students appreciate having options to create and share who they are without having to do a presentation in front of their peers. The use of these tools actually led to more conversations between students and proved to be a fun activity for everyone. Using videos is a good way for students to get to know each other and build connections.

4. Collaborative Google slides. We want to build digital citizenship skills when we are using technology in our classrooms, and what better way than to have students working together in a collaborative space such as Google slides? Create a template and have students to add their own individual slide to the presentation. They can share

FIGURE 6.8 Adobe Spark Spanish II story about childhood dog

> some icons of their favorite activities, a family photo, or a video clip, whatever it is that they can fit onto one slide that will help people get to know who they are. When it's all completed, you have a slideshow of your class that you can always go back and look at throughout the year. A fun way to see how things have changed and the relationships that have formed during that time. There are many other ways to use the same concept of collaborating with Google Slides. We've used it for activities like project-based learning and genius hour and even transferred our Google slides into a Nearpod presentation for an interactive lesson!

For students, having a space to interact with us and classmates makes a difference. These are just a few ideas that gives them the chance to share learning in a way that meets them where they are. We need to create spaces where we can keep learning going and be able to check in with our students because this will be vital. Especially for when our in-person social interactions may be limited, it is critical that we find ways for students to engage in meaningful experiences that promote the development of social-emotional learning skills and empower them to connect regardless of the learning space. We have an opportunity to innovate and reimagine learning as we embrace each new year and each school day.

As educators, we need to make sure that we are connected with classrooms from around the world. When we use technology to make this happen, it not only greatly benefits our work professionally, but it offers so many possibilities for our students. When we model the development of global collaborations for students and involve them more in the design of enriching learning opportunities, we empower them to not only build their target language skills, but also social emotional learning skills and in particular, develop greater cultural and global awareness. Setting up these collaborations does not take too much time at all. You just need to start with one of the options or reach out to your networks. Here are a few additional ideas that might be of interest.

> **Zee Ann Poerio,**
>
> St. Louise de Marillac Catholic School,
> STREAM Teacher K-8 and Exploratory Latin Grades 7 & 8,
> Pittsburgh, PA
>
> A good opportunity for students to practice their language skills is by creating morning announcements for the school. Have students create an announcement to talk about the weather or an event that is happening in school and to talk about it first in English and then say it again in the target language. Depending on the digital tools available, this can even be done with a ticker scrolling at the bottom of the screen with some of the words in Spanish or perhaps use some different features like text boxes or emojis in the background to help with translation. This can be a great way to give students some authentic practice and also increase the interest of other students in learning a different language.

I really like Zee's idea, and I think that it can even be fun if students were to create a weather forecast, a special announcement, an advertisement or any type of broadcast to share not just with students and the school community but to collaborate with other classrooms globally to exchange the news broadcast. Depending on the tools available, students can even work together on creating broadcasts to exchange between their schools. What a way to promote global collaboration and social awareness, by applying and building skills together in the target language!

From Fiama

We started with a project with the Sustainable Development Goals in a world group of teachers. Each of us had a specific goal assigned and we had to design a project to collaborate in the fight for it. To help us, we decided to first work with our students about the world they live in, what we can do to protect and help our world, to live in a better and more equal place, for every human being, animals and plants. This project allowed us to work with global connections and to learn about different situations around the world. I was so excited because of it!

Beyond Our Classroom Walls: The World Is Our Classroom

Beyond teaching the content, we need to offer students learning experiences in different learning spaces so that they have time to explore and build the skills that they will need when they leave our schools. There are strategies and tools that we can use to help students create global connections, learn about the Sustainable Development Goals (SDGs) and build cultural and global awareness. These experiences will empower students to look for problems or challenges locally and globally, brainstorm solutions, and focus more on learning as a process.

Like Fiama, I enjoyed learning about the SDGS from my students and their specific interests during our PBL experiences. Students explored topics of personal interest and developed

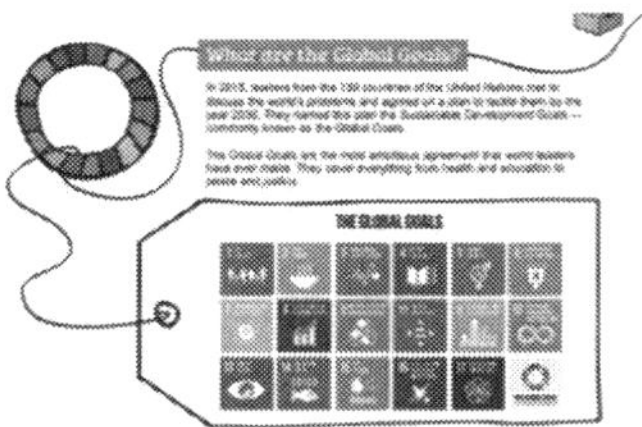

FIGURE 6.9 Fiama's PBL Project with SDGs

> **Luis Oliveira**
>
> One of my yearly goals for my English Learners is giving them opportunities to connect with the world. I want them to learn with the world so that they can become familiar with global perspectives, cultures, and be exposed to different ways of thinking. I use several digital tools to achieve this goal. They include:
>
> - Skype in the Classroom activities such as Mystery Skype, Virtual Field Trips, and Guest Speakers offer my students opportunities to learn about the world without leaving the classroom. We have participated in the Microsoft Learning Connections (Skype-a-thon) every year.
> - Flipgrid, Wakelet and Buncee are my choices because they give the students a voice that can be shared with others. One example was our participation in the Global Write activities. Students were given the choice of using Flipgrid, Wakelet or Buncee to produce their writing topics. This differentiation was very important because of the different levels of English proficiency. My newcomer students preferred Buncee while the intermediate and advanced students chose Wakelet and Flipgrid depending on their comfort with the oral language.

empathy as they learned and applied their language knowledge to real-world learning experiences.

As my class engaged in PBL, we added more to it with each passing year, and at the end of the second year we had our first Skype call with the students and teacher in Argentina. My students were very excited to have that opportunity to talk with their Argentine pen pals. After an entire school year building relationships with them and learning from each other, it was a powerful collaboration. They were seeing their friends in real-life, or as close as it gets, for the first time. There was so much excitement, and it was a culmination of a year of learning and connecting. For me, it was great to be able to interact with the other students and also to finally meet face-to-face with the teacher that I had been planning with throughout the two prior years.

The benefits of bringing these opportunities into our classroom are not just for our students. These opportunities help us to continue to expand our own knowledge and build our awareness so that we truly can bring in the most beneficial, real-world learning experiences for our students that will motivate them to keep learning. It adds value in what they are doing in the classroom

FIGURE 6.10 End of the year with a Skype meeting for the first time with PBL friends in Argentina

and hopefully inspires them to continue their learning journeys!

Music has been integral in my classroom and can be used in many ways. Try teaching about a grammar topic with some popular music or have students write their own lyrics even! I also love this idea from Karina del Castillo!

There are a lot of great choices for helping students to learn about the world around them and connect with other students too. Another fun activity that we did was plan travel for the students from Argentina and Spain to come

Kristen Lyon

My classroom is very music centered. We participate in Señor Ashby's Locura de Marzo, Lococtubre, and follow the Latin Grammys annually. As we listen to songs by various artists, we explore cultures, countries, and communities. Music and music videos allow a view to other parts of the world. Students often then follow their favorite artists on Twitter, Instagram, etc.

Karina del Castillo

One of the best projects in our virtual school year was the "Traveling Tale" *https://bevansjoel.wixsite.com/travellingtales*. My fifth graders learned how to communicate and collaborate with one another thanks to this amazing initiative from Joel Bevans. The main idea is to create a story with the participation of children around the world. It's amazing!

and visit us in Pittsburgh. My students took the lead and, using Google Slides, collaboratively planned a trip, with each student having a specific, self-designated role in the process.

Once the slides were ready, we used the Nearpod Chrome extension to transfer the Google Slides into an interactive Nearpod lesson so that they could add in some virtual field trips, videos and other activities to learn about the interests of the "travelers." We "assigned" the Nearpod lesson to the students from Argentina, who experienced what it would be like to come to Pittsburgh and immerse a bit more in the learning experience. The Spanish IV students were excited to review the responses from their Nearpod lesson, and what made it even better is that the students in Argentina created a trip for them too.

Students teaching each other about where they live and exchanging information using technology through a more interactive and immersive learning experience made a big impact on all students. To be able to build their language skills and SEL skills by working together, setting goals and building social awareness was a truly beneficial and meaningful learning activity for them all. It was also a chance to teach about technology and experience something new together. A trip to Pittsburgh and a trip to Buenos Aires that promoted global collaboration and language learning was a highlight for all students that year.

Here are some experiences to consider from Fiama Liaudat:

We have so many choices available to us to for creating global connections. Sometimes it can be done simply by leveraging audio or video tools so that we can exchange

> Fiama Liaudat
>
> One of the things we did last year was create Virtual Field Trips to our countries (Argentina and Colombia). I learned how to do it using different Google tools like Google Slides, Google Earth, Google Forms, and also other platforms like YouTube. We added in a lot of animated images, videos, map links and we "traveled" through our computers to the main places in Argentina and Colombia. It was AWESOME! It was a great way to have students connect with other places and cultures! Technology allowed us to do a Virtual Cultural Exchange using Google Meet with a group of students from Argentina. Our kids really enjoyed it. It's one of the best benefits of technology: you can create connections around the world just sitting behind your screen!

ideas or set up a space to communicate. It can be something that's done asynchronously or synchronously, that helps us to work with differences in time zones and school schedules, especially as we transition or expand with our learning spaces. It's important to have multiple possibilities to promote global collaboration and connections for our students that help them to understand the world around them by connecting in authentic and meaningful ways.

Final Points to Remember

1. Think about *your* classroom. What do your students need? What is missing? Work together with your students to brainstorm and try new ideas.
2. Pick one new idea or tool to start with. Try it and then reflect on the benefits before taking the next step. Remember not to overwhelm yourself or your students.
3. Push yourself to do something entirely different than what you have been doing in your classroom. To innovate only requires something new!
4. Remember that innovation does not require technology. Try something new or do something a little bit differently. It just takes a minor tweak!
5. Don't worry about making mistakes. It is all part of learning and a good model for our students.
6. Keep learning, reflecting and sharing. Connect with other educators, ask questions, share ideas and tell your story!